Spirit of the Warhorse

Kitty Silverwings

An Appaloosa Story

By Patti Ansuini

Spirit of the Warhorse
Kitty Silverwings, An Appaloosa Story
by Patti Ansuini

Printed in the United States of America

ISBN 9781628711851

www.xulonpress.com

Kitty Silverwings

A filly born into
Treacherous gloom
The end was Imminent
So they assumed

A Spirit Kindred through
Chiefs of the Ages
The wisdom of Fire
Silently rages

The Courage of Tribes
Facing certain death
Will fight to the end
With every last breath

The strength of an oak
Bending in the wind
From the depths of her soul
The healing begins

As gentle and sweet
As the cool morning breeze
She speaks to her master
Through faith of undying needs

As soft as the quiet
In the dark of the night
The master that touched her
Set her wings for flight

Born a rose in winter
Blossomed upon the snow
As deep as the stars
With impeccable glow

A prayer Scribbled
With absolute perfection
Colours of Silver
A glistening reflection

Toni Ansuini© '93

Much has been written about the human-animal bond. From the Nez Perce Indians and following through the author's life. Kitty Silverwings is a book that exemplifies that special connection that many of us find with the horses in our lives. This is a story of courage and perseverance. There is something about a horse that can lift your spirit and allows one to face daunting adversity.

Richard McCormick VMD
Lori Kayashima DVM
Attending Veterinarians,
Valley Animal Hospital

For those who might be cynical when it comes to miracles, the true story of Kitty Silverwings, a royally bred Appaloosa mare, might change your mind. Born with multiple life threatening defects on the Rocking A Ranch in Morgan Hill, California, her owner Patti Ansuini was advised by her veterinarians that the humane thing to do would be to euthanize the chestnut blanketed filly immediately. Ansuini, who says she doesn't hope for miracles, she counts on them, refused to give up and spent the next three months sleeping in the filly's stall, helping her stand to nurse, bandaging legs, dressing wounds and providing physical and moral support when all efforts seemed lost. For the next three years, Ansuini filmed the filly's battle against the odds. Today, many veterinary colleges have a copy in their library to teach students that it is possible for a higher power to intervene and make the seemingly impossible, possible. If you love horses, or just an inspiring read, you will enjoy this well-written, compelling story of love, courage and dogged determination.

Darrell Dodds,
Publisher, Western Horseman magazine

The following statements are excerpts taken from letters received during the first week of November, 1996. The letters were received in response to a letter and video documenting the Kitty Silverwings saga.

Thanks for your video of "Kitty Silverwings." It has been placed in our video library and is available for faculty, students and staff to view at their convenience. Once again, thank you for sharing your story with us and the best of luck.

James L. Voss, D.V.M., M.S.
Dean, Colorado State University

You have documented a remarkable story that documents hope, tenacity, and even heroism on behalf of both you and your Appaloosa foal, Kitty Silverwings. Your video is a visible story of the finest type of interaction between humans and animals in a collaborative relationship which somehow overcame seemingly insurmountable odds. I hope that by your example, succeeding classes of veterinary students will be informed and encouraged to practice their profession with full regard for animal welfare and the value of the human-animal bond.

V. E. Valli, DVM
Dean, University of Illinois
At Urbana-Champaign

On behalf of the College of Veterinary Medicine at the University of Florida, I thank you for sharing Kitty Silverwings' story. The wonderful video brought to life her dilemma at birth and her ultimate recovery. She obviously occupies a very important place in your life, as you do in hers. Again, we appreciate your sharing this touching story with us. If we ever want to check in on how Kitty Silverwings is doing, I have a feeling her address will not change unless yours does.

Eleanor M. Green, DVM
Professor and Chair, Chief of Staff
University of Florida

Table of Contents

Dedication

This book is dedicated to;

Richard McCormick VDM
Lori Kayashima DVM

For believing when all others had given up hope

Dwight Summers, Farrier

With a heart of gold and a touch of Magic

And to,

Silverwings

For the most precious loan

Foreword

In telling the story of Kitty Silverwings, Patti Ansuini shares a compelling example of the spiritual bond that can form between humans and horses. Although often hard to explain, the connection is clearly understood through the emotional saga of Kitty and the challenges she faced. Countless horse owners will tell of special moments of understanding, but Ansuini gets deeper and leaves the reader believing in the authenticity of spirits from the past and the power of prayer to whatever form of divinity it is that watches over our animals.

Kitty happens to be an Appaloosa, so that makes for an intriguing tale beyond what it would be if she were "just a horse." The Appaloosa breed has a rich heritage that is tied to the Nez Perce Tribe and the "Palouse" country of Oregon, Washington and Idaho. It is widely accepted that the Nez Perce were serious about selectively breeding horses that were sure-footed and swift enough for hunts and battle, as well as tough enough to last on long treks through the rugged country of the Northwest.

Nearly becoming extinct after the Indian Wars, a group of ranchers and horsemen worked to form a registry and an association dedicated to preserving the colorful breed. The Appaloosa Horse Club, Inc., headquartered in Moscow, Idaho, is proud of its role in documenting pedigrees and promoting a truly versatile equine and quite proud that we are able to celebrate the 75th Anniversary of the organization in 2013/14.

Perhaps the most significant effort of "ApHC" has been the fifty year tradition of sponsoring the Chief Joseph Trail Ride, an annual horseback adventure through a portion of the historic Nez Perce Trail, retracing the "flight to freedom" in 1877. Importantly, young and not-so-young members of the tribe participate in the ride and provide a level of appreciation, humility and harmony that most of us only talk about.

You are hereby officially invited to visit the Palouse, including several stops within the Nez Perce National Historical Park and of course, the Appaloosa Museum and Heritage Center in Moscow, Idaho. We should never ignore or forget the noble contribution of horses, the Native American culture and generations of horse lovers who have sacrificed for the welfare of our equine friends.

Steve Taylor, CEO
Appaloosa Horse Club, Inc.
Moscow, Idaho

Part 1

Spirit of the Warhorse

Chapter One

Little Bird couldn't remember when she'd ever been so cold. It seemed surreal as she continued to break ice from the eddy along the rivers edge. Water was needed at the camp, one of the few remaining things along with roots and berries that were still accessible to her people.

The icy water did little. It could not even slack the thirst of those who needed it most. The smallest sips of the icy water would cause both the oldest and youngest teeth to chatter and would produce shivers so violent that it shook their bones. It was agonizing to see the pain and misery etched in the faces of the most vulnerable of the tribe's members. If only they could have a fire. Without a fire in the camp soon, it was easy to see that they would be the first to lose the battle for survival.

Little Bird looked to the sky and raised her hands in a gesture of prayer; she asked out loud, "how could this happen to my people"? They had always been at peace with the whites and their native neighbors. Never in all of her memory had they not welcomed travelers into their village and throughout their lands. Since she was a young child she recalled that over the years more and more outsiders had come through their ancestral lands but nothing had changed, her people had always befriended strangers, shared their food and helped nurse the injured until they were well enough to move on.

For many years mountain men and hunters from other tribes passing through the Nez Perce lands would tell stories of the great father in Washington sending many thousands of his cavalry to crush the resistant plains tribes into submission. It was said that once subdued, these tribal people had been moved at a great loss of life to lands far away, never again to be seen in their ancestral homelands.

So many times the elders had spoken of these rumors and they would speculate as to what may have become of the missing tribes. They reasoned that this would not be their fate as the Nez Perce people had never caused any trouble among the soldiers or outsiders. Chief's Joseph, Yellow Wolf and Looking Glass had assured most of the elders that they would be left alone in their valleys far away from those tales of the distant wars between the soldiers and the peoples of the plains.

Once the three main Nez Perce bands came to realize that it was true, the Great Chief in Washington, in spite of their treaty, was sending the Calvary to move them unto reservations. A great majority of the young warriors had argued bitterly for war. But Chief Joseph once again convinced them that they had always been at peace, the Chiefs in Washington knew this and that surely nothing bad would come of this situation.

Joseph had gone on to tell them that since the battle of Little Big Horn last summer, their Sioux brothers had wiped out the Cavalry which had only lead to more serious problems for all of the remaining tribes. All things considered, he still didn't believe the current problems would reach the Nez Perce, simply because there was never a time that they hadn't been at peace. No one could say that they hadn't always been friends of the whites. Outside of a few rare misunderstandings, no Nez Perce had ever made war on settlers or soldiers nor had they ever violated their treaty.

All three of the main bands had been holding joint council meetings more often because the people had become very uneasy knowing that the Army may decide from one day to the next, to forcibly remove them from their lands. To incarcerate them on a reservation was unthinkable; the loss of life as they knew it would be intolerable for the Nez Perce.

At the most recent council gathering they had heard from Yellow Wolf, chief of the northern most band. As he stood to speak, all grew silent. Yellow Wolf said that he had spent much time considering their situation and had decided that all three bands of Nez Perce should go north into Canada. They should remain there until the current crisis has passed. He reasoned that once the war was over they would be able to return to their beloved homeland in the Wallowa Valley and go back to their peaceful co-existence with the whites, just as it had always been.

Once Yellow Wolf had finished and sat back down, the council shared their thoughts quietly as they carefully considered his words. No one was prepared, nor would they argue the point with Yellow Wolf. He had always been held in the highest regard by the tribe. Both he and Chief Joseph had an uncanny ability to outsmart the people's adversaries at every turn. In a council meeting just days earlier, Yellow Wolf had already convinced the other tribes, along with Chief Joseph and Chief Looking Glass that their best plan would be to head north to Canada, where the Cavalry would no longer pursue them across the invisible barrier. They would, at last, be safe.

Little Bird at once recalled that only yesterday, Chief Joseph had spoken to Yellow Wolf about the need of the people for rest and to graze the herd that numbered more than 2,000 head of their much coveted Appaloosa horses. The two had mutually decided that the horses should be allowed to stop and graze for a few days, as they would be needed to carry the people and what little remaining possessions they had on this journey. It was unthinkable that they not consider the horses first; they would be unable to hunt or travel if anything were to happen to their horses.

Yellow Wolf had also assured Chief Joseph, that they were at the very least, two days in front of General Howard and that once they'd reached Iskumtselalik Pah, they would be able to catch their breath. They had time to rest; just a day or so is all that would be needed.

Yes, it would be well to rest thought Little Bird, but she felt a mounting fear along with many of the warriors, that they were still in extreme danger. A few of the warriors along with Little Bird's husband, Spotted Horse, felt that they should send out a few riders on the fastest horses in every direction to make certain that the Cavalry was not close.

It was only because of these brave warriors who had been acting as a rear guard in a gorilla type war that had allowed the tribe to out distance the cavalry at every turn. Nevertheless, Yellow Wolf remained certain of his position and was most insistent that they were safe, the riders were unnecessary, they needed rest. After all, the whites did not know this trail, they would be days behind them, they had time.

When they had finally reached Iskumtselalik Pah, a high mountain valley which the whites called Big Hole, a feeling of well being took hold of many of the tribe members. This valley was well known to the Nez Perce hunting parties, they along with a few of the other tribes used the valley as a stop over on their journeys coming and going out to the plains for trading and hunting buffalo.

Spotted Horse had told Little Bird of this camp and that he had been there many times when he was young and full of adventure. How the other warriors who had rested at their camps on their journey, had told him of the buffalo hunts with herds that were so large you could hear them many hours before you could see them. The roaring sound of the unseen herd was that of a great, distant thunder.

When the herd finally appeared it would be in a towering cloud of dust and as they ran by the noise would be so great that it would cause you to cover your ears. It was as if 'The One' had sent his herds from the sky, as they would completely cover the hills in every direction you looked. The herd had no beginning and no end.

Spotted Horse knew when he'd first heard this legend of the buffalo, that this was something he had to do. He immediately realized that he would need a very special horse, a courageous horse above all, that could run among the buffalo during the fiercest hunt or a fearless war pony as he counted coup on his peoples enemies. This would be

24

a horse that none had ever seen. A pony that 'The One' would send to Spotted Horse, he would know this spirit pony when he saw it, he felt it all the way down to the marrow of his bones.

His friends had always laughed at his idea, to think that he could do all things on one pony. Two horses were needed, one to hunt and one to make war, everyone knew that. He would tell his friends of a legend his great grandfather had told him and that his grandfather had been told by his grandfather, of a young brave and his great spirit pony who were powerful hunter's, none could match their agility or speed in times of need. And of the pair's great courage and how they were as swift as the wind when they counted coup on their enemy, none could catch them.

It was said that in the heat of battle, when many warriors thought for sure they'd seen this young brave and his pony fall, only to shout wild war cries' as the pair would ride out of the chaos unscathed. Over generations of retelling the stories of this brave and his great pony they had slipped into legend. Many believed this was the legend that became Crazy Horse in later years.

Spotted Horse didn't see why it wouldn't be possible; somehow he just knew it would be true. Many times he'd seen Appaloosa horses carved and painted on the rocks in some of the most remote valleys and sacred places known to many of the tribes who used these ancient mountain passes. Many other tribes also believed in the legends and were sure it was the Nez Perce's Appaloosa who bore the sacred marks.

Often times the Nez Perce's friends the Crow, the Flatheads and the Sioux would visit on the pretext that they were just passing through, but in reality it was to bargain fiercely for the chance at acquiring one or more of the young Appaloosa horses.

They believed that the spotted horse would keep them from any harm. They had heard that Crazy Horse had said as long as he was on his pony he couldn't be hurt. He too had ridden an Appaloosa and he had never been touched, even when he rode through the bullets of the army that were as thick as rain. Spotted Horse had even heard it said among the travelers that many of the mountain men also believed in the old legends, as they had Appaloosa spots tattooed on their backsides and in so doing believed they could not be harmed.

All at once Little Bird realized she was shivering and made her way to a small outcrop, beneath a weather beaten old pine. There was a small opening that was just large enough to afford her some protection from the wind. She hunkered down and then tightly wrapped herself in the tattered remnant of the blanket that her uncle had given her earlier this day.

As a little warmth began to creep back into her arms and hands, she watched as the sun began it's decent below the mountains ridge. She wondered if her husband Spotted Horse was safe, if he'd found any- thing to eat and if he was warm. That their beloved Shine was well and that she'd carry her husband back home to her safely. Now that they were in the mountains, it would get impossibly cold very quickly once the sun had set.

Chapter Two

Since this running battle had begun, the people had been without fires for heat or cooking for fear that the smoke would give away their position to the pursuing calvary or those witnesses who might see them making their way through the mountain valleys and would give away their position to their relentless enemies. Those they had thought to be long time friends had betrayed them at every turn. Even now, Yellow Wolf insisted that they silence anyone or anything that could betray their presence.

Again, Little Bird became lost in thought. A smile came to her lips as she recalled that day long ago when she was told by a group of excited friends and her family that Spotted Horse, had made it known that he intended to make her his wife. She was elated, this was more than she could have dared hope for. She had always dreamed that Spotted Horse would choose her. He was a great warrior of Chief Joseph's band and the best hunter among all the Nez Perce.

She had many reasons that she loved him from the time they were children. He had always treated her kindly and with a gentle respect. He had always been very generous and would often bring extra meat or fish to those among the tribe that were not able to provide for themselves. She also knew in her heart that Spotted Horse would care for and protect the people at any cost.

He was out there in the night with dozens of the best warriors from all three bands of the Nez Perce. For weeks now this band of warriors had outfoxed and had held back the entire Army under the command of General Otis Howard, one of Washington's top Civil War generals and he had been assigned but one objective; to bring in the Nez Perce.

In another time and place Chief Joseph and his warriors would themselves be celebrated as legend in the annuals of war strategy. They had accomplished, time and again, the seemingly impossible task of keeping the tribes and their horses out of harms way. It was because of their courage and bravery that the people were at this moment within a half days walk of the Canadian border. All they needed this night was for a brief rest before that final trek to the North. It was just so cold and everyone wanted to believe Yellow Wolf, he was so adamant; they had the time.

She began to think about the missionary's stories that Chief Joseph had been told by his father Joseph. How he'd been baptized and according to the missionaries he would now go to heaven when his feet left the earth.

Chief Joseph wasn't certain that he believed in the 'One God' but, he knew that his father, Old Joseph, believed most of what the missionaries had taught him. He had even named his son Joseph, for the very special Christian name he had been given. Chief Joseph wasn't sure that his father truly believed or even if he'd convinced him that the 'One' existed but, he reasoned, it didn't hurt to have more reasons for a faith than less.

Little Bird was now so cold that she was almost afraid to fall asleep. She thought it possible that she might never wake again. Maybe she would find that the 'One's' heaven really did exist. She pulled her knees up to her chest and rested her forehead on her knees.

Little Bird remembered a few more stories some of the elders had shared with her. They believed a great many of the stories that the missionaries had taught them of 'The One God.' They had also heard similar stories among other native people over the years. They didn't like to speak of it in the village for fear that they would be ridiculed. But those who believed would sit and speak in hushed tones of their certainty that 'The One God' would save them at last.

She hoped with all her heart that they were right and that they would be remembered by their people for all time; just as the ancients had never been forgotten by her or her people.

Chapter Three

Little Bird awoke with a start. Her heart was racing, what had she heard? She realized how afraid she was out here alone in the dark night. She trembled as she listened for long minutes. She heard an owl off in a distant pine. That must have been it, just an owl on the hunt. It was so cold, she struggled to readjust the blanket so that it might cover more of her, but there just wasn't enough meager material to do the job.

Wasn't it just yesterday that Shine had been born. The filly had started out so poorly. She came so very close to losing her life before it ever had a chance to even begin.

Many years before Spotted Horse had spent an entire summer trying to capture a wild born Appaloosa that had caught his eye. He patiently worked with the young mare and was well pleased with the way she was working out. In time he had begun to think highly of the mare owing to her willingness to always please him. She was fast, had great stamina, good strong feet and legs and she was very beautiful. His friends and many braves from other tribes agreed with his assessment, but try as they might he just wasn't willing to part with her for any amount of goods that were offered up.

The day came when Spotted Horse thought it would be wise to breed the mare while she was young, just in case something were to happen to her. Yes, he would at the very least have a great son or daughter out of her. He felt fortunate that he already knew who had the greatest stallion he had ever seen and he thought the chances good that the answer would be yes.

He spoke to Chief Joseph the next morning and it was immediately agreed a breeding of Spotted Horses fast, brave mare to Joseph's fine Appaloosa stallion would indeed be an excellent cross.

The stallion was dark as the night with bright white splashes of color on his rump. He had a star that took up most of the space between his eyes. He too, could run like the wind and had a great opinion of himself. You could see it reflected back at you in his eyes.

He would loudly snort to warn all comers who might mistakenly think to invade his territory. He could be heard as far away as the distant hills. As he moved over the ground, he remained suspended in the air, his feet rarely touched ground. He held his tail high in the air as he floated through space with the wind. Anyone witness to this display knew there was no doubting who he thought he was, just the very best in his world.

Spotted Horse had been certain that this would be a great match. Perhaps he would even end up with the spirit pony he had dreamed about in the days of his youth. The way he saw it, maybe the 'One' would send her to him, he had always known it would be another mare and he had kept that secret hope all to himself.

The filly was born during a wild spring storm and owing to the fact that she had been in a very big hurry to come into the world, things just hadn't worked out as well as Spotted Horse had hoped.

Little Bird and Spotted Horse knew that the filly was due anytime and had been keeping her mother near their lodge, but during the night the storm had spooked most of the herd and they, along with the mare had moved off to find better shelter for themselves.

When Spotted Horse and Little Bird found the mare and her newborn filly, they realized immediately that something was terribly wrong with the new foal. She wasn't able to stand, nor had they seen her try to nurse. Her legs were horribly twisted and looked as if each pair came from the center of her body. Little Bird knew that they would have to get the horses back to their lodge so that she might be able to help with the little one.

Spotted Horse wasn't able to hide his disappointment from Little Bird. He told her that he would put the little one out of her misery. Little Bird said they would speak of it later, once they returned to the lodge and had a better look at the baby.

Little Bird was able to keep the small filly alive for the next few days as Spotted Horse had gone to hunt for game and overcome his sorrow. When he returned he had already decided that no matter how Little Bird pleaded, he would finish the sad business with the filly.

Normally after a hunting trip, Spotted Horse would take time to visit with a few of the Elders before retuning to his own lodge and Little Bird. If the hunting had been good he'd share his catch or game with them. But not this day, he went directly to Little Bird to tell her that he had decided that the best thing to do was to put the filly down. He would not be deterred.

Little Bird could not remember the last time she had ever cried, she had no control over the copious tears spilling down her checks. Neither had Spotted Horse ever seen her cry, so it came as a big surprise to both of them. She pleaded passionately with Spotted Horse, "Please she begged, there is a great spirit in this filly, you must not end her life."

He was so surprised by Little Bird's outburst that it stopped him short. He looked into Little Birds pleading eyes and then wrapped his arms around her and held her close.

"Are you sure of this"? "Yes", she had assured him and so it was that Little Bird was to spend many hours each day working with the filly for the first two years of her life."

She had grown tall and strong. She had proved her potential to all those who had been skeptical and especially to Spotted Horse, who never failed to smile every time he watched her kicking up her heels and racing through the meadow.

Once Spotted Horse began training the filly, he realized that she was everything he had imagined. She had the speed of her sire and was lightning quick combined with the courage of a Grizzly Bear. She was stealthy on the hunt and he would return with game when all the other braves had failed to do so.

By the time the filly was four, he had already counted coup on her a dozen or more times. She very quickly became known far and wide by many other tribes to the point that Spotted Horse, kept her next to the lodge to keep an eye on her, lest someone sneak in and steal her during the night. How fortunate he felt that she had returned from near death to become all the things he had ever dreamed of her. He was so grateful to Little Bird for believing in the filly, for seeing her potential when he had in the beginning failed to see it all.

All this time they had referred to the mare as the little one or filly, but now she had earned a name that was a true reflection of who she was and had become. Spotted Horse had been thinking on this for some time and had already decided.

He walked with Little Bird down to the rivers edge and they sat next to each other on a fallen log. Spotted Horse told her of his travels as a young boy with his father to the land of the ancients. "In a very remote part of the Wallowa, there was a place I saw that had many paintings among the deepest parts of the wall edges. The drawings continued into many caves large and small, where our ancient grandfathers had lived too many generations ago to count.

The paintings were of hunts and war and of ponies with the markings of our great Appaloosas. Also, there is another thing I saw there that was amazing. There are streaks in the walls near these drawings that look like ice, but they are not ice. When the sun begins to set high over the canyon rims, the sunlight strikes this not ice and it blinds you so that you have to turn away. It shines as bright as the sun itself."

Spotted Horse continued, "I believe that the mare has been sent to me from our ancient Grandfathers and maybe even the 'One'." I believe her name will be 'Shine' in honor of our ancient grandfathers who came long before. I believe she will live up to her name.

Chapter Four

Little Bird hadn't even realized she'd fallen asleep, now she's waking in terror. Someone had taken a tight hold of her and had clasped his hand over her mouth to keep her from shouting out. In took her long seconds to realize the voice she was hearing whispering in her ear was that of her husband, Spotted Horse. He repeated to her that she remain very still. He explained that he didn't have much time and that he'd slipped back into camp with urgent news.

Once she regained her calm, he quietly told her that it was only a few hours before the light of day would begin and that the Army would capture and strike them down in the early morning light if they didn't act fast.

Yellow Wolf had been so sure of his advice; most of the tribe's members had been convinced of their safe position. But Spotted Horse and a few of the other braves felt uneasy and disobeyed the advice of the elders. Once the camp had settled down for the night they readied their ponies and rode out in different directions to check on the actual position of the Army.

It didn't take them long to find the Army. It was just after midnight when they made first contact. They could see that the soldiers were already packing their tents and gear, getting ready for the forced march into the Nez Perce camp at first light.

Spotted Horse and his group of warriors met at their rendezvous point and shared their own horrifying news. It wasn't General Howard and one Army, it was three separate armies under different commands and they were coming from three different directions.

For a few terrifying moments, there was only stunned silence at their people's hopeless situation. Spotted Horse broke the silence and told them, "As long as we live, we will keep the Army from our camp. If we can give our people a little time, they can get to the border and all will be well with them.

He had quickly explained all this to Little Bird along with the news that Chief Joseph and his old warrior friend, No heart, had already been told and were at this moment moving the herd north. The herd would be safe for the time being. Everyone understood that if they lost the herd, they along with their possessions and freedoms would be lost forever. Without the horses they might as well surrender. There had been so much hardship and suffering already they would not quit, they were too close to their goal to stop now.

He told Little Bird that she must get into camp and wake her sisters and that they get the children and elders moving for the Canadian border quickly. There was so little time left. He understood that they were sick and cold and starving, there were no other choices to be made, for a chance at life, they needed to move and move quickly.

He finished by telling Little Bird that he and the other warriors would do their best to keep the Army from moving down the mountain pass and into camp. He was sure that the other warriors would know by now, that the tribe was on the run. It would give them great courage knowing that every moment they held the Army, the closer the people would be to freedom.

Spotted Horse held back the rest of the news that was weighing heavy on his mind. How each of the braves had agreed that they would do their appointed tasks and then rendezvous in a few hours. Each of them had in absolute silence held up their arms in acknowledgment of the war they were about to make on their enemies and then rode out. They all knew that this would be the last war they would ever fight and for every hour they held the army off the closer their people would get to freedom.

He embraced her tightly, they closed their eyes and for a brief moment rested their foreheads together as if in a final prayer. They both turned away at the same instant to keep the other from seeing the tears that slipped down their checks. They each imagined the other might think the tears a signal of weakness neither wanted the other to see. They both knew that these would be their last moments together in a world that they had shared for most of their young lives. Neither imagined a life without the other.

Spotted Horse jumped aboard Shine and in an instant they were gone from her sight. Just as he had asked, she ran as fast as her legs could carry her to the camp. She found her sisters and told them that she would explain more later, but that now they needed to get the children and elders moving as quickly as possible, they were in grave danger.

They voiced their concerns about their possessions, but Little Bird told them there was not enough time to pack, that the things they absolutely needed would be replaced once they got to Canada.

So the sick, the little children and the elders began to move, but Little Bird could tell they were just too exhausted; many too cold to want to move and most were just far too hungry. They were not willing to move even knowing that they might not live another day. Little Bird looked up to the mountain peaks and could see that the dawn was near.

The people were now scattered between camp and maybe as far as two miles to the north. There had not been enough time. Most felt they were finished, too weak to care too move on.

Little Bird stopped short; she thought she'd heard what sounded like thunder. She continued to strain to hear, and then she heard a horse's death scream. Some of the old travois horses that were still in camp were beginning to spook at the terrifying sounds coming from the pass.

Little Bird was overcome by a horrific feeling of dread. She turned around in time to see one of the camp's travois horses had broken loose from his tether and was coming in her direction. She jumped out in front of the panicked animal and flagged him down, she jumped aboard and gave him a kick and headed for the top of a nearby hill that looked out over the pass that lay in the direction of the Army's advance.

As she topped the hill she could see that the Army was much larger than she had ever imagined. They had canons, the type the army called Mountain Howitzers. They were the source of the terrible thunder. The smoke from the cannons lay heavy along the ground and the air was thick with the acrid smell of black powder and blood. Horses were being cut down and they were screaming wildly like nothing Little Bird had ever heard before.

All at once she saw Spotted Horse and Shine running all out toward the leader of the Army. The entire world seemed to disappear and all she saw was Shine falling as if life were happening in slow motion. She heard Shine's scream and could see Spotted Horse tumble along side Shine.

A loud sob escaped Little Bird as she kicked her mount into a run. All she knew is that she needed to get to her husband and Shine. She ran half the distance to where she'd seen them fall and her horse screamed, took several more faltering strides, then fell with her.

Little Bird was aware that her side ached as if she were being stung by a hive of angry bees, but she had to stay on her feet, she had to get to Spotted Horse. She was having trouble seeing and she was so very tired, where were they. Then, for the briefest of moments, a small breeze cleared away the fog of war and there, mere feet in front of her lay Spotted Horse and Shine.

She felt very faint and was having trouble keeping her balance. She had to make it the final few feet. Then all at once she fell to her knees. Her tears came in a great rush as she forced her knees to carry her the final distance. She reached out her hand and softly stroked her husband's cheek. She turned her head and softly laid her right hand on Shine's still warm neck. Both were gone. She looked to the sky and beckoned to 'The One' in a final prayer. Please hear me Grandfather, my One True God; please do not let them be lost forever. They are the legend that Spotted Horse dreamed of.

As Little Bird spoke her final prayerful words, a fatal bullet found its mark and Little Bird fell forward between her beloved husband and their spirit horse Shine. Her last conscious thoughts were of a dream that Spotted Horse had once told her. He had had a vision, that one day Shine would carry them both into heaven's land of legend.

As Little Bird released her last breath, the dark clouds began to roil wildly, the rain came in great torrents. The lightening flashed and the thunder rolled.

Part II

Living the Legend

Chapter One

No one could ever deny that the day I was born, I had arrived with an all consuming passion for Equus Caballus, better known as the magnificent horse. His DNA was embedded so deeply in my psyche that it ran all the way to the very depths to my soul.

My mother had always insisted that it was the Gospel truth and would cite as proof the fact that I hadn't uttered a single intelligible word until I was nearly two years old. She had expressed her grave concerns to the family that there may be something seriously wrong with a child of my age, who hadn't had a single thing to say. Most of the family assured her that she was needlessly worried; it was simply owing to the fact that I didn't have anything of interest worth bloviating about. Her concerns were whisked away as wheat chaff one early fall afternoon.

All had been quiet that lazy afternoon. Mom was working in the kitchen and I was perched on a chair at the kitchen table happily working away on my favorite coloring book. As if on cue, I suddenly stopped, dropped the crayons and climbed down from my chair and made a bee line to my mother's side where she was standing at the kitchen counter. I tugged at her apron and waited patiently for her to give me an audience. She dropped her jaw in utter amazement as I began speaking in full sentences on a subject that would one day become the absolute apex of my universe.

As my mother re-told the story over the years, it had turned out to be the actual subject matter itself that had rocketed this event into the Twilight Zone for her. I had broken my silence to talk to her about horses and gave voice to my first query as to when she thought she might be able to bring one home for me.

To her knowledge no one in the area owned a horse, nor could I have ever seen one as we lived in the city and there wasn't a neighbor in any direction with a backyard horse. We were far too poor to own a television set, so it all remained a great mystery for many years to come.

At the time mom had written it off as one of those strange, quisquous events that no one could ever truly hope to explain, let alone understand. Only God had the answers and He wasn't talking at the moment.

I'd often wondered that if at a very young age we don't already have some subtle inkling of God's plan for our lives. In my case it did appear that God had most certainly posted notice to my family very early on.

Growing up, I had never given up on the dream of possessing the horse that I so passionately desired. Every time my family moved into a new home, I'd point out that the backyard was exactly the right size to accommodate a horse. At one point my dad had told me that when I grew up, I'd be able to get that horse I'd bugged them endlessly for. He had even gone as far as to tell me that he didn't see any reason that I should stop at just one. The way he saw it, I should have at the very least one horse for each day of the week.

As I listened to him I remember thinking how absolutely brilliant his idea was. I just hoped that somehow fate would intercede on my behalf and that my parents would come up with one long before I grew up. To be grown up sounded like eons into the future, and using fast track kid logic, that sounded way too far down the road to suit me.

Time slipped by, other things had become more important in my life. In my twenties, like so many of my friends, it seemed I too had set my childhood dreams aside. Time's a very relative commodity. I had promised myself that I would never lose that love of the horse and would one day very soon, do something about it. But the older I got, the swifter that river rolled on.

One day I was struck by the realization that I hadn't really ever forgotten my mysterious love of the horse who still occupied my sweetest dreams. I became aware that he still freely roamed the valleys and misty mountains in my minds eye. He had over the years taken on every conceivable color and coat pattern. But, one thing had always remained constant; 'my horse' had bold war paint and a fierce spirit.

As a young girl I could imagine him on the crest of a high hill, he stood defying the wind as it pulled and snatched at his wildly blowing mane and spiraling war feathers. My spirit pony was the most magnificent creature I could ever have hoped to behold; the vision could literally take my breath away.

Chapter Two

By the time I reached my early thirties I hadn't given much thought to my war pony. He and his hill felt as though they had faded far off to a very distant range. He had given way to the long hours of work that both my husband Pat and I were putting in. We were raising our two young sons which had become a full time task to be sure.

When the boys were still pretty young, Pat and I had bought a small outboard motor boat. We had many great adventures hauling that boat on camping and fishing trips. Mainly the trips were just us and our boys, but from time to time we'd take along a few of their 'best' friends. As they all grew older we realized what a powerful sales pitch young boys can muster. In a relatively short period of time they had managed to persuade management to buy a ski boat. Their sales pitch included points specific as to the reasons for a flashy paint job and included extra special emphasis on the idea that not just any old ski boat would work for this crew. Oh no, this boat had to be strong enough to easily haul up five skiers, at speed.

As we were to find out, they had all been right about those good times they'd promised. We had more fun than one family deserved and the years literally flew by. Then out of the blue, the morning dawned on Pat and I when we'd shared an alarming epiphany. We both realized that the boys where approaching driving age and they would fully expect to be able to take that jet boat out by themselves. As we saw it, once they had that coveted driver's license in hand they would be relentless about that ski boat.

We pondered the known 'truths' with respect to teenage boys and decided that without a doubt the first thing the boys would throw in that boat would be the beer, everything else would be incidental. But the source of our main concern was the fact that this particular jet boat had a fire breathing, bored and balanced, five hundred plus horsepower engine onboard. We could see the flashing red lights all the way from there.

So we decided to sell the jet boat and find a nice lumbering day cruiser that we could do a little deep sea fishing on or maybe spend some time on leisure bay and Delta cruises. The boys would be much less likely to kill themselves with such a rig.

Pat had gone ahead and set up a few appointments for he and I to take a look at a few boats on and around the Stockton and Sacramento waterways. As we headed up the freeway towards Delta country, we had traveled all of thirty minutes from home, when we came to the first set of the bay area foothills and we began to climb. As we rounded the first curve, cruising along in the slow lane was a one ton Ford Pickup hauling a two horse trailer.

I looked long and hard at that rig and then said more to myself than to Pat, "I would trade a thousand boats for that rig right now." At the time I would've bet that he hadn't heard a word of what I'd said or my long sigh of resignation. The sad feeling that thought had brought over me felt as if a heavy blanket had been thrown over me. I realized in that moment that from where I sat this day, my war pony was now lost to me forever.

Here I was at what many considered the half way point in my life and I was about to find out that my giving up on a dream didn't necessarily make it so. As it turned out, God had been listening to me all along and he had grand plans for me and my long awaited war pony.

Chapter Three

It was exactly one week later to the day that my husband presented me with my first horse. I cried tears of absolute joy for days.

I put everything I had into learning how to ride. I practiced six days a week come rain or shine. As I saw it, I had a lifetime of learning to catch up on. Now that I had my first horse I began to gravitate toward people who had horses and were very serious about showing them.

About one year after I began riding, I felt confident enough to enter my Appaloosa mare Scribbles, in a few Western Pleasure classes at the prestigious Grand National Rodeo and Horse Show in San Francisco. The exhibitors who customarily entered the classes at this show come from all the western states and then some. At the time, this San Francisco event was considered the show of shows.

At dark thirty on the morning of the show my best friend Ruthie had picked up Scribbles and I and we began the hour and a half drive up to the City.

Ruthie had actually come to my rescue a few weeks earlier when the cowboy/trainer who I'd been taking lessons from during the past six months had quit me just two weeks prior to the show. He had decided that he didn't believe Scribbles was nearly pretty or talented enough to win the big open classes at such a prestigious show. He figured he didn't need the embarrassment of losing that show riding Scribbles in that pair of open classes. No, there was nothing I could say to make him change his mind, he was sure that he didn't have a chance in a million of winning with her.

I got pretty upset with him; to think that he'd quit me that close to the show, not to mention that I'd already paid all of our entry fees. So I decided I'd brass it out and told him I'd go it alone. He just laughed and wished me lots of luck.

Ruthie pulled up to the ranch at about 4:00 am the morning of the show. She helped me load up all my tack and I collected Scribbles from the barn and loaded her in the trailer and we headed out.

We hadn't gotten that far up the northbound freeway when I began telling Ruthie that I couldn't believe I'd had the audacity to actually go ahead with the insane idea of showing without my trainer at the Grand National. To begin to think that I, an unknown, could show against so many of the top trainers, what could I have been thinking? I was so overwrought that I was chewing up her Rolaids by the handfuls just to quell the earthquake going on in stomach. Told her she should probably hang a u-turn as soon as possible and haul Scribbles and I right back home. As I saw it, bare minimum, we'd need another two weeks just to get bare bones ready to show.

Then figuratively speaking, a lightening bolt hit the truck. A series of the craziest things began happening. Country Western super star George Straight's, 'Amarillo By Morning,' began to play on a local radio station Ruthie just happened to have randomly tuned in.

It got our attention in that it seemed pretty strange that we were hearing this particular song on a station that had been playing jazz moments before. Then considering how upset I was about the trip it did get our attention.

It was 'unusual' in that Ruthie and I were very big fans of George Strait to begin with and this wasn't a Country Western station that we'd ever heard about. Over the past year we'd memorized verbatim three of George Straight's biggest hits at the time and would sing them at designated times when we rode out into the foothill areas of a nearby rugged park wilderness area.

When things would get especially edgy and that had happened in a relatively quick hurry on more than a few of our rides. What usually tipped us off to any danger was when we'd hear the sounds of something heavy breaking branches and snapping brush in the narrow canyon areas where the foothills began and the wild sows were known to be raising their babies. We'd even heard that there were Puma's about, but lucky for us we never caught sight of each other that we'd ever been aware of.

The 'Cowgirl Up' tactic we employed was to start singing one of the three George Straight songs we'd memorized. The ploy had never failed us, as the horses never did spook. We had actually fooled them into thinking that we were in complete control of the situation. Even the wild pigs bought into our tactic and never did charge us. Of course once we were out of harms way we'd laugh like loons and talk about how nuts that was and we were.

Then a second bolt smacked that truck. 'Amarillo By Morning' finishes and without even a short commercial break our second George Straight song, 'All My Ex's Live In Texas' begins to play. We both start singing and from time to time let loose with 'that's amazing' and 'wow, what are the odds.'

'All My Ex's Live In Texas,' finishes up and I looked at Ruthie and said, "Wow! Now that was pretty strange." I no sooner got that out when the third of 'our' three songs begins to play. This time it's 'Does Fort Worth Ever Cross Your Mind,' by now we're really singing; okay by now we're not actually singing as much as belting out that song. The only way to describe what was going on in that truck was purely joyful.

One would think that, that was all the coincidence you could possibly imagine happening during the course of your entire lifetime. If we'd have settled for that line of reason we'd have been dead wrong. Our morning was only just beginning.

By the time the third song had finished I was grinning so broadly my face ached. I looked over at Ruthie and said, "Today is going to be an incredible day, I feel it in my bones." We were absolutely giddy the rest of the way to the San Francisco. We shared one more high five as we rolled into the parking lot of the Cow Palace. We had arrived.

Chapter Four

By entering weeks earlier, I remembered that I had to scramble to the office to remove my trainers name and add mine as the new pilot aboard Scribbles. As I scratched the trainers name and added mine to the entry it gave me pause to reflect, a real short reflection at that. I was still grinning like a fool, picked up my number and was out the show office door like a shot.

I was now entered in three classes in the Western Pleasure Division; my first class was scheduled to be the non-professionals class. Next would come the two open division classes that my trainer was originally going to ride. The first of which was Senior Western Pleasure for horses five and older and the grand finale of the show would be the Stakes Class. The stakes class offered a decent cash purse to the top three winners. Both the Senior and the Stakes classes are normally the professional horse trainer's exclusive turf; rarely do non professional riders enter for the purely obvious reasons.

Now that I had my entry number in hand I headed back to the stall where Ruthie and Scribbles were waiting. Ruthie pinned my number to the back of my shirt and asked how I was feeling. I just flashed a grin and we started tacking up Scribbles.

Once I was on board, I headed Scribbles in the general direction of the warm up pen. I don't exactly know what I'd call my mood at that point, just kept telling myself that this was going to be a great day, the signs were certainly in play and what kinda' odds you'd get betting that our three George Strait courage anthems would play in an uninterrupted row. Unheard of, something wild was up for sure.

My first class was called to the arena, Non Pro Western Pleasure. Scribbles almost felt like she was loose to me, but she toted me around that noisy arena like a trooper. We finished the second direction and were called into the center of the arena. They began calling the placings starting with the last place finisher being called first then on down to the first place champion called last. The logic is to keep the crowd in suspense and to see how close they had called the class themselves. In a big draw show like the Grand National there are many sponsors who contribute all the prizes and cash awards, so it can take a while before they finally announce the Champions.

For me it seemed I'd been sitting out there in the center of that pen for hours. I piddled with Scribbles mane and told her she'd been great and thanked her for the good ride. I didn't ever look up at the grandstands as I was praying for all I was worth. I was focused on a prayer and if God gave me the Non Pro win, I would never ask for another thing in my life. When the announcer finished up with the sponsors he paused briefly one more time, at this point I'd stopped breathing and hoped I didn't fall off my horse before he announced the winner, "And our Grand National Appaloosa Non Pro Champion is . . . I came near jumping off Scribbles, they had just called my number followed by my name!

I could barely contain myself, I just kept repeating, "Holy cats, I just can't believe it . . . can you believe it? Thank You GOD"!

My next scheduled class was Senior Western Pleasure and there were several classes in front of that so I parked Scribbles over in a small area near the bucking chutes and waited with some of the trainers who would be riding in the Senior class with me.

Some of them I knew and they congratulated me on my non pro win. They didn't hide their surprise when I told them that I would be showing in the Senior class. They asked me what happened to my trainer. I simply told them that he couldn't make it.

We had been sitting there long enough that Scribbles finally cocked a hind foot and proceeded to nap. Horses don't need long naps to get refreshed. When my next class, Senior Pleasure was called into the arena Scribbles was posting notice that she felt pretty good and that this was a bit on the boring side. It did occur to me that she might do something, might not be an idle threat, then on the other hand, not one, but we'd heard 'ALL THREE SONGS,' nope; we'd be good.

Scribbles got a little goosey feeling here and there, but it wasn't something anybody without a keen eye would have caught. We made it around the pen and I was extremely grateful. I wasn't sure it was a great ride as I knew that's what I would have needed to beat the best trainers.

Again, the announcer took plenty of heart wrenching time to get to the placings. I thought that if Scribbles and I had, had a great ride we might've earned a third place ribbon. I genuinely didn't expect there was anyway an unknown non-pro from down the road, California, could beat some of the top professional trainers. When the third place winner was announced and it wasn't Scribbles, I reached up, smoothed Scribbles mane and told her it's OK, we won the Non Pro what more could I possibly ask.

At this point, I'm just waiting for my chance to leave the arena once the Champion is named. Next came the Reserve Champion announcement. It was one of the trainers I knew from California. I congratulated him as he walked by. The next thing I realize is that I can hear Ruthie up in the grandstands and she's screaming so loud I can hear her all the way down to the arena floor. No way did I just hear that; over the booming speaker system they were announcing that Scribbles and I had just won the Senior Class!

There was no stopping them. I was scrubbing tears off my face with the cuff of my shirt. This was Xanadu! Again, all I could think or say was this had to be some kind of fairy tale, but then I looked skyward and said, "Thank You God"!

The last class was immediately after our Senior class win. I no sooner got Scribbles through the gate when she posts warning to me. She's getting tired and is threatening to run off. Aw, c'mon Scribbles just one more class. 'No,' she tells me, 'I'm done and there is nothing you can do to stop me.' Now that had me a little worried as I was beginning to believe her, but I kept pleading that she just hang on, this was the big one.

Once the judge asked for the reverse of direction and a cadence change in the new direction Scribbles literally blows off the rail and heads for the opposite wall in front of the bucking chutes. The entire audience made a very loud collective gasp and the judge responds by first looking up at the audience, then turns around to see what could have happened in the arena to illicit such a crowd response and sees nothing. By the time she'd turned around Scribbles had already reached the opposite rail and was doing her impression of the perfect pleasure horse. To me it felt like the judge had to be the only person in the building that missed the Scribbles horse boogie! Absolutely another gift from the Boss!

I do admit that by this time my insides felt like Jell-O, it just seemed like one crazy dream after another. Even now, I figured it was okay, how could I be upset we'd already won the Non Pro and the Senior, how could I be so selfish?

The class mercifully ended and we're all called once again, to the middle of the arena to await the award placings. I actually had the temerity to expect I might get a placing in the top ten. When they cruised right on past tenth, ninth, eighth then seventh and they missed us, I expected that I should be so grateful that we'd won the first two and that was that. Again it was just a waiting game until I could leave the arena and go celebrate our two out of three wins!

There were so many sponsors for the Champion of the Open Stakes class it took an extra amount of time. This time I was awake when they called out the Horses name that had won the Grand Champion Stakes Class and I was sitting on her! I reached forward and threw my arms around her neck and thanked her, I thanked God and cried!

By the time the sun had set over San Francisco Bay that evening, the most miraculous of the unimaginable scenarios that could have possibly happened did! Scribbles and I had won all three classes at the Grand National!

It really was some kind of fairy tale! Paparazzi types were taking our picture; there was a reporter from a leading equine magazine asking questions about me and wanted to know all about my great mare Scribbles.

To add to this wild dreamscape there was a couple from Florida who followed me around offering up a blank check for Scribbles. They insisted that I go ahead and just fill in any amount that I felt would be a fair price for the mare.

When Scribbles and I were called to the presentation area of the arena to receive our awards, I had done a wild drowning man wave at Ruthie, that she should come on down! People continued to crowd around the three of us as the awards were presented. What a scene that was as Ruthie and I threaded our way through the crowd and were eventually able to lead Scribbles on out of the building.

Scribbles had a very large championship ribbon around her neck and one of, if not the largest blue ribbons I had ever seen hanging from her bridle. I too was loaded down with the shows top awards and ended up having to share the load with Ruthie. As we walked out of the Cow Palace that evening we'd gone about half the distance to the truck and trailer when Ruthie stopped, set down the loot and buried her face in Scribbles mane and gave her a bear hug. Then she turns to me and flashes a Cheshire cat grin and gives me a little shove and says, "See, I knew you could do it all along!"

Ruthie later told me that her voice was hoarse and her face hurt for days after all that wild cheering and crazy woman grinning. I had always believed that anything was possible, but deep down would always hint at limits. That was before the Cow Palace happened; that day's events had made a blazing run over the border and ran headlong into the heart of divine intervention!

That was the day that I learned that it takes a barrel full of courage, a truckload of want to and a soaring faith that will not be denied!

As it turned out, that was just the beginning for Scribbles and me. For the next couple of years I hauled Scribbles to open and all breed Appaloosa circuit shows in and around California. We ended up winning many year end high point State and National championship titles. At the end of that time I'd decided to retire her. She was a grand girl and she'd given me so many thrilling adventures that I couldn't in my wildest dreams have ever imagined.

Scribbles was such an honest mare, she had never withheld an ounce of everything she had to give in the performance arena. She was breathtaking to behold in the show arena and in so doing made me look like I actually knew what I was doing. Truth be told, at the time if I could manage to keep from falling off and if I gave her all the correct cue's we would consistently win, she turned out to be that good.

Chapter Five

When I retired Scribbles from the show arena my hope was to be able to breed Scribbles to a stallion worthy of her formidable talents and abilities. Maybe I reasoned, I had been so blessed to have been able to have ridden and shown a great champion, why not continue Scribbles linage with a son or daughter. But, the main reason for retiring her early was that I felt she had without a doubt earned that right. No one could have argued that she hadn't earned the rest, that and a mountain of carrots to boot.

Scribbles had proven to me that there truly was a legacy of legends in the heart of the Appaloosa horse. She had made all those wild childhood dreams of having a horse come flooding back. Scribbles had carried me far beyond a realm that I could have ever even imagined.

There had been those times with her, when I swear to you I could feel that wild wind blow down through the decades. It had reached out to me all the way from that long ago hill top, right out of a little girl's land of dreams.

Part III

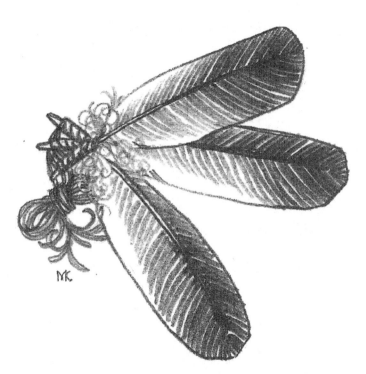

Kitty Silverwings, An Appaloosa Story

Chapter One

It had been more than a week now since I began dogging almost every move poor old Scribbles had made. I say poor because she had become exceedingly uncomfortable, especially this past week. Her ribs were sprung so far out that it had caused her normal body width to look nearly double in size. Each big move she made such as walking at a speed that she'd actually get somewhere, or if she were to lie down or get up; any of these movements would produce long drawn out grunts and groans.

Throughout the week I'd been telling everyone who inquired as to Scribbles and what they referred to as her 'M.I.A.' foal status that I was pretty confident that Scribbles was going to have her foal just any time now. But then I'd thought that all week long. All the usual signs of imminent birth had been present throughout the entire week. But today, now there was just something different about today. I was sure today was the day.

During all this extra time I'd spend with Scribbles I actually believed that I had Scribbles number when in reality it was Scribbles who held all the aces. You'd have to get up pretty early in the morning to fool any one of the old broodmares. I was of course laboring under the assumption that I knew Scribbles well enough to recognize the looks she would cast my way, as if to say, "Aren't you ever going to leave?

I won't have the baby while you're in here hanging around for Pete's sake." I would even grin at her and tell her right out loud that I was on to her ploy.

Mares instinctively will have their babies in the wee hours of the morning because it's the least likely time a predator will be able to find the vulnerable mare and baby. Horses and in particular their foals, are at the top of just about every predators preferred choice menu. Being aware of Scribble's basic instincts didn't change a thing for me, I was determined that I wasn't going to leave Scribbles to her own devices and risk missing the birth. I had been anticipating the birth of this particular foal for months now. To say that I was excited would truly have been the understatement of the year.

So far this spring we'd already had a pretty strange foaling season, omens not withstanding. My cutting horse mare Levi, had, had her foal just days before in the most unexpected way. I fed the mares their evening meal at 5:00 and then headed back into the house to fix dinner. I'd probably spent no more than an hour and a half from start to finish in the house when I headed back out to the barn.

Levi was in the number one stall so that once you'd cleared the barn door the first long face you'd see was Levi. Several evenings ago when I came through the door I could see that Levi was still at the feeder and munching away at what was left of her hay. Once she realized that I'd entered the barn she jerked her head up and flashed me an intense look, then just as quickly decided I wasn't up to anything that involved her and went right back to scrounging up the last little bits of her hay.

All seemed quiet so I figured there was no time like the present to muck out the horse stalls for the last time today. I grabbed the manure cart and tools then headed for Levi's stall. I slid her stall door open and SURPRISE! Guess who showed up for dinner? Levi had to have decided that she would like some company for dinner. She had to have lain down and given birth to her foal the minute I'd walked out that barn door. I couldn't have been gone for more than an hour and a half tops and here was her new filly already up and nursing. That was just so incredibly amazing; no fuss easy foaling. Wow, wouldn't every horse breeding operation in the world give just about anything for guaranteed no fuss, easy foaling? I'd never had a mare do that, nor had I ever heard of it happening in my circle of friends!

I finished mucking out all the stalls, put the cart and tools away then walked back out to the front barn door. I looked toward the east foothills and noticed that a long line of ominous looking clouds were beginning to literally roil up over the hill tops. The longer I watched this strange spectacle the weirder it was getting. The clouds had begun to tower up into massive thunderheads as I watched. This was all happening during the very last rays of a beautiful sunset. I couldn't help but think this entire scene was looking a lot like some kind of a high tech FX scene in a major Hollywood production. Weird.

The storm was definitely heading in our direction. From time to time I could see flashes of lightening followed minutes later by a deep rumbling thunder. I couldn't help but think what a freak storm this was for California at any time of year. It brought to mind the summer thunder storms I'd seen in the Midwest. I was a little surprised to be feeling apprehensive. It wasn't that I felt spooked, but still the look of it did conjure up thoughts of a superstition or two. For one, I couldn't help but wonder what our American Indian legends might have to say regarding the future prospects of foals born during freaky thunder storms.

Finally came back to reality and decided that it might be a real good idea to make a full circuit of the barn area and make sure the animals were faring well with this strange storm coming in. A couple of the dogs seemed a bit nervous with the thunder, but in no time they'd all seemed to have settled down for the night.

I went back into the barn and climbed up to my perch at the top of the hay bales expecting to resume my nightly version of the 'I don't want to miss Scribbles foal' vigil.

Scribbles had finished most of her hay and had backed into the furthest corner of her stall. From this distance it sure looked like she was hawking me even more intensely. After long minutes of our mutual stare down she cocked a hind leg, dropped her head and neck a tad lower and appeared to have dozed off. From inside the barn I could hear the storm was definitely coming in. The wind had picked up and from time to time flashes of lightening would light up the outside paddocks. The ominous sounding thunder was getting much closer and shivering the barn's timbers.

I turned my attention back to Scribbles. She seemed completely unaffected by the stunningly weird weather just outside her paddock doors. She looked surprisingly comfortable all things considered and continued to doze.

There is an old cowboy adage that tells of mares and their apparent control over when and where they're comfortable having their foals. The more I thought about it, the more I couldn't imagine Scribbles having her baby during a thunder storm. At the same time I was starting to feel pretty tired and was having trouble keeping my eyes open. I thought that I might as well go back to the house and cat nap throughout this night's vigil. Once inside I grabbed a couple of pillows, an old quilt and threw them on the couch. I scrounged up my small travel alarm clock with the plan of setting it to wake me hourly so that I wouldn't miss one minute of the on going, 'Scribbles vigil of progress', or the lack thereof.

The plan had worked pretty well the first few hourly checks, but it was getting tougher and tougher for me to force myself up off the couch and out to the barn. It seemed that my past weeks nightly vigils were catching up with me. I slept right on through the 1:00 am alarm. At about 4:00 am I woke bolt upright to the sound of a driving rain. I looked over at the glowing clock face and yelped out a noisy "Oh no"! I jerked on my boots, grabbed my raincoat and ran all the way out to the barn.

The ground outside the barn had gotten a little slick and soupy, so I slowed down then stopped just short of the barn door. I caught my breath, then forced myself to calm down before entering the barn. Once inside I looked for and couldn't see Scribbles over the top of the stall wall so immediately knew she was down in the straw. It was akin to a chant as I repeated, "Oh no, please, please, don't let me have missed it," When I reached Scribbles stall door, I slowly slid it open. With her back pushed right up tight up against the stall door lay Scribble's brand new foal. In that instant my first thoughts were of my excitement at seeing Scribbles foal and realizing what a beautiful, characteristically patterned filly she was.

Once I'd recovered from the initial shock of finding the baby had been born, the very next thought smacked me right between the eyes. Why was Scribbles the entire distance of the foaling stall; a good twenty four feet, away from her brand new foal? Now that had me more than a little concerned. Scribbles and her foals have always been virtually inseparable from the moment of their birth until they become independent of Scribbles on their own. There was never any doubt about it, Scribbles had always loved being a mom. This stall scene amounted to a mental red flag for me, something was definitely amiss.

I quietly entered the stall by circling around behind the little one. Once I'd entered the stall, Scribbles immediately got to her feet and softly nickered to her foal. The foal spontaneously answered and made a strong attempt to rise and stand. I was relatively sure that the filly had probably been born during the past half hour or so as she was still fairly wet and part of her birth sack was covering a small portion of her hind quarters. I mentally pushed back on the idea of there being a problem.

I decided that I was overreacting, that the birth was still fairly recent and that mom and baby just needed more time to bond with each other. I left the stall as quietly as I'd come in and climbed back up to my perch in the hay.

No sooner had I settled in when I heard the rustle of straw as the filly attempted to stand. Just as quickly she fell backwards against the stall door and slid back down into the straw. She put forth mighty efforts time and again as she attempted to make it to a standing position. It was beginning to look like sheer desperation. Each time she had tried the crashes were becoming more and more brutal. I was becoming very afraid for her.

Something was horribly wrong. Scribbles too was beginning to show real signs of agitation with her foals lack of progress and began to forcefully push on the fillies withers' with her muzzle. She would nicker to the filly which would produce even more desperate attempts by the foal. Nothing Scribbles had tried had gotten her foal any closer to standing than attempts the filly had made on her own.

I climbed down from the hay and watched the pair from directly over the stall wall. I watched this heart wrenching drama for a few more minutes. I began to worry that Scribbles may in her desperate attempt to get the foal up, cause even more trauma to the obviously impaired foals already desperate situation. The real worry now was that the filly was becoming extremely tired from her epic battle to stand. I also knew that if she didn't nurse soon she could also miss out on the mare's first nutrient rich milk which was the colostrum, absolutely critical to the foal's immune system.

Once again I entered the stall and hunkered down in the hay near the door. I could now see that the filly looked to have something seriously wrong with her right front leg. I'd been watching this heart breaking drama for the better part of an hour already. When I thought about how long I'd been in the house, close to four hours, I realized that I really had no idea of when the filly had actually been born. It could very well have been hours before.

I decided that she needed all the help she could get and she needed it right now! I very quietly moved toward the filly than got down on my knees next to her and stroked her velvety neck and muzzle. She looked up at me with a soft quiet eye then lifted her head from the straw. I continued to gently stroke her neck and shoulder and then began to speak just above a whisper to her. I promised her that it was going to be alright, that I would never let anything bad ever happen to her from this moment on and that I would be with her always.

I examined her leg more closely and noticed that both of her front legs had extremely contracted tendons, but the real damage seemed to be her right front leg and foot. Her leg looked to be just ligament and bone. Each time she had tried to stand her right leg had flopped uselessly around, as if all the tendons and ligaments had been cut. To make matters even worse, the bottom of her right foot was practically pasted to the back of her pastern.

Our biggest problem at the moment was that the filly was extremely exhausted. I decided that it would probably be best to keep her quiet and let her rest until she decided to make another serious attempt on her own. I prayed that we still had enough time; that she wouldn't quit.

Scribbles had remained very quiet while I'd examined her foal, as if she understood what was going on and that I was only trying to help. When Scribbles decided a short time later that enough was enough, we were running out of time, we needed to get the filly up and nursing. So once again Scribbles began to call to her foal. In immediate response the filly rolled up on her sternum and nickered back acknowledging her mother's call. The spirit of the moment moved me to tears; this beautiful filly was such a fighter, she was going to try to stand again, only this time she was going to make it! I was determined to do whatever it took to keep her on her feet.

I bolstered up her right side to make up for that useless right leg and together we slowly made our way over to the Scribbles. Scribbles kept up the 'coach-like' nickering the entire length of our transit across that stall. Once we reached Scribbles side, I slid my hand under the filly's lower jaw and guided her head to her momma's udder. She suckled greedily for a few short minutes then wanted to lie back down. I took great heart and uttered a thankful prayer for what had been her first time suckling.

Chapter Two

Each time the filly rose and nursed it seemed her stamina was beginning to improve and would make it a few extra minutes. When she would finish nursing I would help her to lie back down which proved to be as equally challenging as getting up. Once she was back down in the straw she would fall instantly asleep. She was so exhausted, but at least now I felt we had hope on our side.

Earlier, during our second nursing session; the filly had fallen deeply asleep and Scribbles had finally quieted down, I had taken that opportunity to put in a call to my vet's exchange. I left a message with his answering service that I'd had a problem foal born during the night. I didn't feel that she was in imminent danger at the moment, but would need to speak to him first thing in the morning.

Both of my equine Vets arrived together at first light to examine the filly. They spent long minutes looking the filly over and would from time to time speak to each other in hushed tones as they conferred as to the filly's ills. Once they'd completed their examination they turned to me to discuss what they felt the situation was. It was at that moment that I realized I'd been holding my breath. I was so afraid of what they might or might not say.

They had concurred; the filly had many problems the worst being a severed radial nerve in her right front leg. For all intents and purposes the filly only had three useful legs. To compound her problems the prognosis was even more dire as she also lacked muscle tissue over her right shoulder and forearm. Then of course there were the extremely contracted tendons. The vets felt she most probably wouldn't live out the week. They suggested immediate euthanasia would probably be the best thing we could do for her.

Teary eyed, I went back into the stall and knelt down next to the filly. I laid my hand on her now dry, fuzzy neck and she opened her eyes and looked up at me as if right on cue. I stared long moments into those soft brown eyes and I saw the hope of life. She was not ready to quit nor would I. As long as she was willing to continue to put up the good fight I would keep the promise I had made to her.

I stood and walked back to the stall door where the vets were waiting for my decision. They were most sympathetic and explained to me that the odds of a three legged horse surviving beyond six weeks with the added growth and weight would be an absolute impossibility. They went on to explain that the youngster would rapidly deteriorate, then eventually lie down too exhausted to go on. I knew that my family would also wish for nothing more than to spare both the filly and I the pain of what they believed was the inevitable certainty of her death.

Once again I turned back to the filly and knelt down in the straw beside her. To look upon her at that moment, she seemed to be absolutely at peace. Each time she opened her eyes and looked back at me she looked like a curious youngster who simply wondered what all the excitement was about. Her gaze was sure and calm; it was in that instant I made the decision to trust her with her own life. I turned back toward the stall door where the vets and my husband were now standing and let them know my decision.

They all seemed very dismayed. They suggested a period of six weeks, no more; if there wasn't significant improvement that they could see, she would be lost.

Chapter Three

At twelve hours of age the filly had already acquired a new roommate or second mom depending on who you asked. I had piled plenty of new straw throughout the stall. I had also banked straw half way up each stall wall, which to be honest was more for my comfort than the fillies. The stall was now home to her equine mom and a most interesting human that ministered to the balance problems.

In a few short days I came to realize how smart the filly was. She seemed to know when to rest and ever since that first terrible night, she'd never overdone it again. She never tried to frisk or jump like most 'normal' foals. She constantly napped when she wasn't nursing which thus far had worked out to be every two hours or so.

Scribbles had through all of this unnatural foaling season, been accepting of all the extra attention. The three of us had many visitors during the filly's first few weeks of life. Most well intentioned friends and family members thought the she was far too lethargic and would tell me that any fool could see that she was going to die. From all quarters, the advice persisted, you should have her put her down and that I was only prolonging the inevitable. Never did the filly hint at quitting, nor would I waiver in my decision to fight this battle with her.

I did understand that my close friends and family honestly believed what they were saying. They felt certain that they had proof positive by way of the vets prognosis, the fillies survival just wasn't a possibility. I knew that their intentions were simply to save me from the pain of fighting a losing battle. They were so sincere in their pleadings that I felt compelled to quit working and spend all my time caring for the filly. I wouldn't say that I didn't trust anyone, it's just that I could envision arriving home and having a family member console me with the news that the foal had perished while I was at work. My parents had even gotten to the point that they were now refusing to come by the ranch for their weekly visits as my care of the foal bordered on cruelty. My closet friends constantly urged me to finish it for our own good.

If I hadn't spent those three months living in the barn with the filly, I would have missed learning that we are blessed with some of life's greatest treasures. Sitting in the straw next to the filly as she slept, I began noticing things that I'd missed before; the beautiful rhythmic sound of a spring rain falling on the barn roof. Deep in the night the sound of night birds and owls on the hunt or the absolute calming stillness of the barn when all the horses have been fed and were peacefully munching hay as they settled in for the night. The heralds of the dawn, the songbirds whose melodies I had never really taken notice of before. All this time I failed to realize that my own barn was a virtual doorway to heaven.

Most nights the barn cats would wander in and lie in the straw next to the filly and me. The filly had always shown a great interest in the cats and would always rise up on her sternum to touch them when they'd wander over to us. There were times when the filly would look as if she were sleeping soundly and I, not wanting to disturb her would quietly call to the barn cats, "here kitty, kitty", and the fillies eyes would open wide and sparkle with keen interest. She'd then nuzzle me as if to say yes; yes by all means call them in. It seemed to me she liked the name. It was an Ah Ha moment when it finally dawned on me that she'd actually chosen her own name. From that day forward Kitty it would be.

Chapter Four

It was during the second week of Kitty's life that the skin at the point of her elbow and another small area at the point of her shoulder started to die off. The tissue beneath began to collapse in both of these areas. Abscesses were beginning to form.

Unable to handle the situation alone, I called my vet back and had the dead skin and underlying abscessed tissue excised at the elbow. I don't know why or how, but felt we should leave the shoulder alone for the time being.

Once the tissue had been removed the abscess at her elbow had been laid open to the joint, a very dangerous condition for a newborn.

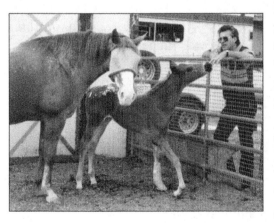

Foals are born with next to no immune system to speak of and what little resistance to disease they do acquire is through the mother's first milk, the colostrum.

Once again my vet shook his head and said that it was baffling to contemplate all the filly's ills. This time he explained that the fear of a lethal infection was a distinct probability especially compounded with his earlier prognosis.

Incredibly we managed to keep a bandage on her abscessed elbow for the entire week which had helped to keep the wound clean. The scary looking area at the point of her shoulder miraculously started to heal on it's own without the slightest intervention.

One week after the open abscess on Kitty's elbow had begun it was decided that it should be unwrapped and allowed to 'air.' We slowly removed the tape and peeled back the bandage, I held my breath, said a prayer and if in instant answer, it was. The wound was dry; it looked healthy and was healing at break neck speed.

Each day Kitty gained an infinitesimal amount more controlled motion in her leg. She was starting to pick up her shoulder by tiny degrees and beginning to use the face of her ankle to walk on. To look at her head on, her sternum was twisted dramatically to the left side of her body and her right elbow had dropped down almost as low as her left knee, but still she would try for all she was worth to use her feeble leg. With each attempt her goal seemed to be able to stand a little more upright. It was exhausting work and she slept many hours. Visitors still came by and said they sure weren't seeing what I was. She still looked pretty hopeless to them.

At five weeks Kitty was able to push her bum leg forward by two or three inches and rest the tip of her toe on solid earth. It wasn't a pose she could hold for very long and her efforts were nothing short of Herculean, but it was something our visitors were beginning to take notice of. I also noticed that the requests for her immediate termination were starting to become less and less opined.

Kitty's vet held a tremendous amount of admiration for her spirited attempts at a normal life and would drop in about three times a week to see how we were doing and what I thought we might try. He admitted that he was still completely perplexed by what ailed the filly. As far as he could ascertain foals born with problems of this magnitude are usually aborted or still born. Kitty was of great interest and curiosity to him. He openly admitted that he still held out little hope, but was genuinely amazed at the little one's bull dog tenacity.

At approximately eight weeks, Kitty's radial nerve had begun to 're-attach' itself. She moved very slowly and pushed and pointed 'that' leg as if it were full of 'nitro.' At every labored step she would heave her body upward to complete one forward step. It was incredibly painful to watch, as she worked with every fiber of her being to accomplish the task at hand. When she wanted to reverse direction she would pivot her entire body around her left front leg and I feared she would destroy her 'good' front leg in the process. It was pure agony for me to watch her efforts, but I just couldn't; nor wouldn't give up. She was waging nothing short of a heroic battle for her life and I absolutely believed in her.

After one particularly heart wrenching day, I began to weaken and started questioning the wisdom of our battle. It was late afternoon and Kitty had just lain down from a dramatic walk across the paddock that was purely gut wrenching to watch. I couldn't stop the tears and I began to pray; "Please Jesus help us. I'm not asking to bring back the dead or save the world; You brought Lazarus back with your touch", I leaned over and placed my hands on the soundly sleeping Kitty's forearm and shoulder. My heart was breaking and I was sobbing pitifully, "Please Lord, touch me and through me please heal Kitty. It isn't much, she's just a little filly, but she's fighting for all she's worth. Please I beg you, help us."

I was totally spent and painfully aware that our six week deadline was very nearly up. It seemed the general consensus of opinion from just about everyone, that the simple facts were that they just weren't seeing the progress I'd kept assuring them that there was. I decided I'd sleep in the house that night. I was so completely dispirited that it seemed hardly worth my next breath.

The next morning I awoke at dawn and headed for the barn. It was a cool, gray misty morning as I made my way to the barn. I could barely make out the silhouette of what had to be Kitty standing in the outside paddock doorway. It struck me that she looked as if she were waiting for me. As I drew closer, I realized how I never ceased to marvel at what a beautiful baby she was and at this moment I thought she looked absolutely magical standing there all squared up; ON ALL FOUR FEET! I stopped dead in my tracks, slowly set down the bucket of grain I was carrying and waited to see what was going to happen next.

Kitty continued to stare back at me as if to make sure that I was indeed paying attention. Very slowly she pivoted her entire body so that she was facing directly toward me. In the next instant I became a witness to the very miracle I had prayed for. In a purposeful slow, halting walk, she came across the paddock directly to me. I was overjoyed, she could walk. I don't remember walking over to the paddock fence, but the next thing I knew I was on my knees and had reached through the rails and was hugging her for all she was worth and I cried like a baby and thanked God for all I was worth.

Chapter Five

It was simply because Kitty had never used her right foot that it had become grossly mal-formed and taken on the shape of a small wooden peg. With every forward step she took, she had learned that she had to raise her shoulder up and then out in an exaggerated move in order to make the least little bit of headway. It was a painful looking proposition. The time had come to call in my farrier, I knew he'd know how to handle this very special situation for Kitty.

I'd had the same farrier for many years and knew and completely trusted his work. He was also very aware of what I had been going through with Kitty. Once I explained her specific problems to him he promised to be out early the next morning and take a look at what we could do for her.

As promised he arrived the next morning and right away admitted that he'd been moved by Kitty's undeniable spirit and indomitable courage. He felt confident that he could help her, but explained it was definitely going to take 'some time' to fix her problems. He reasoned that she was obviously tolerating some discomfort, but if we were to try to do too much, to soon with her, it could be more than she would be able to bear. No point in adding extra hurdles for Kitty at this point, she had already come so far.

He went on to explain that the tendons and ligaments had to be slowly corrected and to do that would take small amounts of rasping on her tiny hoof on a week by week basis.

True to his word, every week he dropped in and spent a great deal of time studying her and how she was using her crippled leg and foot. There were some weeks he ran the hoof rasp just once on just one side of her foot. There were times when Kitty would react as if he'd stung her with an electric cattle prod.

Once the farrier had attained a little balance with her foot, I began turning she and Scribbles out into a small sand arena so that she could frisk and play. There were times when I'd worried that she might tear

down any progress we'd made thus far, but the idea that she could be building strength, muscle and bone far outweighed the negatives. As she played, she would put on a stunningly powerful display of her zeal for life. Those first turnouts with Kitty amounted to some of the greatest blessings in itself for me and any visitors to have been fortunate enough to have witnessed them. I cannot tell you the times that we stood just outside the arena wall with tear stained checks apologizing to each other for being such 'softies'.

Again, over a very short period of time Kitty had proven how incredibly smart and patient she was with herself. She had figured out that if she kept her hind quarters deep underneath herself she could lift her weaker front end off the ground, pivot on he hind quarters and run off in the opposite direction. She became very adept at this amazing maneuver and used it often. When she became tired she would use both front legs together and could race around the paddock area with what looked like an officially breed recognized, three legged gait.

There were a few times when Kitty had gained far too much forward speed and her crippled leg just wouldn't be able keep up the pace. It would cause her to drag her bad leg beneath herself. She wouldn't be able to keep that up for long when she'd eventually land a hind foot on that trailing front leg and foot. Visually, it looked to have the same effect as if she had been dragging a rope. Once she landed a hind foot on that front leg she would either come to a dead stop or slow it down to a snails pace and hobble around in a small circle just long enough to ease the ouch. Each time something like this would happen she appeared to consider what had just happened. Once I began turning her out in a larger pen that was big enough to gain some real speed, she learned very quickly what exactly it was that she could or couldn't do.

At five months of age Kitty's vet was still dropping by, but it had become much less often, about once every two or three weeks. On one such occasion Dr. Rich had dropped by to check Kitty's progress.

He and I walked out to the two acre pasture that Kitty had been turned out into earlier in the day. She spotted us from out back and came charging up to see what was going on. The vet commented that he never ceased to be amazed at her miraculous recovery and he'd tell me so each time he saw her. I pointed out to him how well she was coming along and that she was now using her bum leg and foot consistently.

I confessed that even I felt that she still looked pretty frail, but for all the world, I expected that she was looking like she just might achieve a normal leg and foot.

He examined Kitty's shoulder and forearm. It still looked skeletal and had absolutely no discernable muscle tissue. He pointed out to me that if you looked at Kitty head on, she was incredibly narrow. Her right side, shoulder and forearm were shrunken and very concave. On the other hand, her left side, shoulder and forearm were well muscled and convex. I admitted that yes, she did indeed look as if she'd been put together with spare parts.

The vet looked from Kitty back to me and read my unspoken thought. "She will never regenerate the missing muscle tissue. You cannot regenerate what you're not born with. The best you can ever hope for is that she will be strong enough for you to use as a broodmare. She will never be capable of being ridden."

I considered his words a moment and almost felt a pang of guilt because here I stood in receipt of one genuine miracle and I'm thinking I would receive another. After carefully considering my words for the briefest of moments, I plowed full speed ahead and pitched all caution right out the window, looked Dr. Rich in eye and said, "If I've learned one thing from Kitty, it's that I shouldn't count on miracles, I've absolutely come to rely on them."

His face lit up with a very wide grin and he left it at that.

Chapter Six

As a yearling, I wouldn't say that Kitty had achieved perfection, but if you were to stand directly in front of her you'd immediately notice that she had once again defied all the odds and achieved the impossible.

She had achieved complete symmetry. The muscling in her arm and shoulder had been built from a medically diagnosed 'zero.' There was absolutely no discernable difference between her right and left sides.

Visitors who stopped by the ranch who were completely unaware of Kitty's history, were always surprised by Kitty's story. Most were surprised and said she certainly didn't appear to have ever had anything amiss.

It was truly a God send that we began video taping Kitty at twelve hours of age. Without the proof of video tape many thought we were grossly exaggerating the facts of Kitty's tribulations. Outside of a few scars that had resulted from her days of walking on the face of her right pastern, a scar that ran the entire length of her right hoof and the telltale site of her elbow abscess, which remains hidden from view by a curious looking cowlick.

The veterinary community at large was at a total loss for an explanation as to what had happened, and or how it ever was resolved; the operative word used and used often was miracle.

Chapter Seven

As a long yearling Kitty had gained more than enough strength and stamina to start some light training. Not only was she gaining in strength, but also in size.

Basically, this was going to be the time she needed to learn some very basic manners especially with regard to being halter broke. That meant that I should be able to leave her tied to a hitching post and expect her and the post to still be there when I got back.

Kitty was an amazingly quick study and was honest to a fault in her intent at aiming to please. The few times we had a difference of opinion it was usually something she had to patiently teach me.

One of the very first things I realized about Kitty was that she was far smarter than most horses are ever given credit for. All this time I'd bought into the idea that horses just weren't that smart. It was starting to look like those smart trainers I'd been listening too were the ones lacking in intellect. Maybe it would turn out that Kitty and her mom Scribbles weren't the exception to the rule, maybe most horses were this smart.

All these years I'd heard trainers explain to their novice riders that horses, generally speaking, weren't the brightest critters in God's animal kingdom. Working with Kitty during her early years, I'd learned that what I thought I knew just had to be dead wrong.

Most horses probably were almost as smart as Kitty. There were times when Kitty could be scary smart and I'd wonder who was training who. Being that smart has it's drawbacks for sure. It could complicate things when it came to trying to figure out who she really was.

Before I ever started Kitty's training I wanted to know what she was like when she was on her own. Was she brave, timid, aggressive, to know this I'd have to watch her from a vantage point she didn't suspect I was watching. If Kitty spotted me watching her she'd immediately stop what she was doing, trot on over and expect that the "go ahead scratch my sweet spots" session was about to commence. I suspected that if I wanted to get anything seriously figured out about her I'd definitely have to do it undercover.

As it turned out the spying idea worked out to be a boon in learning what Kitty was really all about. I was surprised to learn that she spent most of her daily turnout either investigating or harassing the unfortunates that happened to venture into her pasture. She rarely missed a thing that went on in her world. She was neither timid nor overly aggressive. She would immediately zero in on any and all things that had the misfortune of walking, crawling or flying into her free space. She hadn't yet reached the boredom stage for the time being, but I was certain that with all that smart and given a bit more time, she couldn't be far off from becoming a first class juvenile delinquent. As smart as she was, I figured she'd most certainly welcome a change and some challenge to her daily routine.

Once Kitty's training began in earnest we hit our first mental brick wall. Even though her physical wounds appeared to be completely healed, she'd had formed the habits and mindset of one who believes that they're permanently crippled.

For two years running, I worked Kitty on the lunge line and did a lot of in hand work. The lunge line work helped her to more easily learn her gaits; the walk, jog, trot, lope and canter. Lunging also helped to build her strength and stamina, but the thing I had to guard against was letting Kitty get bored and lunging can get real boring. The last thing

I wanted to do was to put so much pressure on Kitty that I would end up souring her on our training sessions.

Always keeping that in mind, she worked on same or similar movements but the training routines had to be changed everyday. Doing the in hand work with Kitty was at close quarters and I was able to reward her for the right moves immediately. She began to regard all the in hand work as rewards.

In-hand work always consisted of a series of maneuvers through an obstacle course made of round, ground poles and railroad ties. She learned to do walk over's, back through's, turns on the fore and back hands and side passing. Using the obstacle course had helped to break the monotony of lunging. The obstacles also contributed to building muscle, coordination and strength. Another real advantage to the obstacles was that while all this seemingly incidental work was going on she was also learning my riding cues. The method to my madness was that if my idea worked then she would be well aware of the cues before I ever climbed aboard.

One of the greatest things I'd have to say about Kitty's training regimes was that she showed me how much she loved being praised. She always responded to praise from me in any and all forms. Just knowing that about her had me heaping it on thick at any and all her attempts at picking a leg up a little higher or her persistence on achieving a particularly difficult back through. She would continually push herself to accomplish what for her was a mountain of a walk-over or a challenging side pass. She genuinely relished the praise and attention and it seemed that she'd try that much harder to do what I was asking for a bear hug and that exuberant 'atta' girl from me!

Her patience and persistence were awe inspiring. Those who witnessed her attempts and successes always marveled that she seemed so aware of the need to conquer the training challenges put before her. Like most good show and working horses, Kitty was especially fond of the times she spent in the barn being groomed, where I would tell her all my secrets and more than occasionally throw in sincere hugs. She would doze blissfully or flutter her eyes lashes and sigh as I brushed her coat to a high shine or braided her tail up in colorful rags.

At three years of age, Kitty was started under saddle. Like a duck to water comes to mind. In the beginning she seemed more than a little dubious as to whether or not she would be able to handle an onboard pilot. To actually be expected to tote me around an arena for any length of time seemed a confusing idea. But in the end all the ground work we'd put in had definitely made a powerful impression on her. There was also that Kitty extra special asset that was never to be overlooked or underestimated and that was that war horse spirit of hers. That alone had always made her powerfully game to try.

For months we put in quiet rides that went a long way in convincing her that she really could hold up her 'crippled' shoulder and that once crippled leg underneath herself in some relatively tight turns. She still needed some convincing that she really could lope into and out of a perfectly square corner. This final hurdle was beginning to turn into the serious brick wall I'd prayed we'd never hit.

We had worked on this maneuver for most of the spring of her third year. I was beginning to lose hope that I would ever be able to convince her that she really could do it. It was getting to the point that she wasn't even willing to give it a try. Each time I'd ask, she'd quit and act as if it was all me, my short comings for not remembering she was crippled.

Late one afternoon I decided that today was going to be the day, we'd either get that tight 'L' turn down or we'd leave it behind us forever as a no can do maneuver. Acting as if I knew she would, I asked Kitty several different times to lope into the corner and fully expected her to make an effort at the turn. I could feel that she was getting pretty tired of my pushing the point and was beginning to refuse even considering the request. Each time I'd ask she'd flat refuse me. After she'd refused multiple more times, I climbed down and pulled her bridle off, put her halter on, loosened her saddle cinch and tied her to a hitching post and walked away from her.

I wandered around the property feeling sorry for the both of us and sat under a shade tree and contemplated our remaining choices. I had been completely out of her sight but hadn't been gone for more than twenty minutes when I rounded a corner and she welcomed me back with a nicker. I walked back to her, but rather than untie her and take her back to the barn and unsaddle her, I tightened up her cinch, then pulled her bridle back on and climbed back aboard.

I just sat there quiet as a stone. I had absolutely no plan consciously in mind as to what would happen next. Kitty was a little curious as to my strange behavior and kept flicking her ears back at me then she too eventually settled for just standing quietly.

I'd finally made up my mind. I decided that it just didn't really matter to me whether or not Kitty could make that turn. So what! She was already a shining example of what a champion was all about. To me she was by any definition a genuine world beater! She had in her short life already accomplished nothing short of the miraculous. What more could I possibly ask of her? I felt incredibly selfish for ever pushing her to make that turn at all. The real truth of it was that I'd been forever blessed by simply having her in my life.

I walked Kitty back out to the arena intending to just lope for a few minutes then get off and put her up. As we began loping, we headed down the long side of the arena and just before we got to the corner I turned her loose on a long rein and decided to let her do whatever she wanted to do with it and with that she loped squarely into the corner, lifted her right shoulder and made the perfect square turn and loped back out into the flat. I let her go maybe three strides down the rail then very quietly stopped her. I immediately dismounted and threw my arms around her neck and told her that I knew she had it in her to do it. I piled on the praise like I'd never done it before, "What a fine, gorgeous, super smart equine you are. I am button bustin' proud of you." She put her head over my shoulder and pulled me even closer in what amounted to her version of hugging me back, fluttered her lashes like a Hollywood starlet and licked her lips like crazy, which was Kitty's "WOW, I get it and can you believe it? I did it!"

What a glorious day! This had worked out to be one of those blessed Kitty moments that could and did turn a routine day's simple ride into, one of our thrill rides of our lifetime together.

Chapter Eight

By the end of the summer of Kitty's three year old year, she had built up a fair amount of stamina and was able to lope a time or two around an averaged sized arena. She had developed cadence and could, I was sure, make a decent showing in a western pleasure class. I had even begun loading her into my trailer and hauling her varying

distances to friend's ranches where I had started working her in new areas just to get her used to the idea of working and staying relaxed away from home.

Mentally she was always with me on our trips down the road. If something startled or had her worried she would always defer to me and wait for a response. One word and a pat on her neck from me and she would completely relax and wait for the next command. I couldn't imagine life with a horse being any better than this.

Lately, I'd found myself contemplating the idea of showing Kitty at a small regional horse show. Maybe just enter her in a class or two. The thought was wildly fantastical for me to even be considering. Then the whole idea of it would make me feel as though I was expecting far too much of Kitty. But, on the other hand, she seemed to love her 'work' and she was for sure moving so well. In a daydream world it all seemed so possible. I couldn't imagine that she wouldn't be anything short of a super star in the show pen. To contemplate the road we'd already traveled it seemed that nothing sounded impossible.

I phoned a friend of mine who worked as a professional horse trainer in southern California. I explained my desire to possibly enter a horse show with Kitty that had been scheduled for the coming weekend in his area. I asked if he wouldn't mind if I came by with Kitty, as I would very much like to show him what Kitty had achieved and talked more about the tremendous progress we'd made. I mentioned that I'd also appreciate his opinion on how he thought Kitty and I might fare in the show world in general. He urged me to load her up, come on down and he offered to do what he could for us.

It was a five hour drive to our destination in Southern California. Kitty rode as if she'd been hauled her entire life. She never let out a peep or seemed the least bit anxious. As for me, I couldn't remember ever being as nervous as I was on that trip to southern California. If I asked myself once, I begged the question what seemed a hundred times; what in the world did I think I was doing? Why was I dragging Kitty all the way down here?

By the time we arrived at my friend's ranch it was early evening which meant that I had just time enough to get Kitty bedded down in a stall for the night. I was going to have to wait until morning to ride and gauge Kitty's emotional state after what I figured was an epic five hour trailer ride for her. There were also plenty of strange horses and her new digs that sure might have put her off some. This was an awful lot to take in for a sheltered filly that'd never been away from home.

That evening sleeping sure hadn't been easy for me. I had gotten up and checked on Kitty many times during my restless night. At first light I was up, dressed and outside ready for the day. I pulled Kitty out of the stall and got her tacked up. The trainer made an appearance a short time later and immediately found a lofty vantage point on the top rail of the arena fence as I began putting Kitty through her paces. I couldn't read much in his facial expressions and he sure didn't say much more than comment that he felt Kitty still didn't look real strong. He did mention that he thought I was probably right about now being a good time to start her out at something. He, like everyone else was totally taken with her survival story. But then reiterated, as he had more than a few other times, that he thought she probably wouldn't ever make much of a show horse reasoning that she would never be strong enough.

I'd always valued his opinion and with that in mind I respectfully listened to his appraisal of Kitty's future prospects. But the way I saw it, Kitty and I had already come this far, why not go to the show. Who knows I told him, she has always put forth her best efforts and is one very game Appaloosa filly. We came all this way, I think I'll just go ahead and give her a try.

Early the next morning we were on the road and headed to our first show. My friend the trainer, had other clients and horses that he'd intended to coach or exhibit at this same event, so it had been decided that we should all caravan to the show. My friend had, at the last minute decided that he'd like to tag along with Kitty and I during the two hour haul to the show grounds.

California's Central valley is known for its extremely arid, blazing hot, Indian summers. By eight in morning it was already hot enough that I was beginning to notice that there were heat mirages forming near the far horizon. I couldn't help but think that this was going to be a scorcher of a day as I continued up the road and into the eastern foothills.

It wasn't long before I began to notice the mirages weren't just at the horizon line, that they seemed to be starting to rise up along the very edge of the highway. They shimmered off into the distance, out through the miles of vineyards and turned into flickering walls of sparkling gray haze on the horizon. As we climbed through the foothills a slight breeze had apparently kicked up and started to lift and flutter the shiny silver and magenta Mylar streamers that had been hooked to the top of tall poles throughout the vineyards. They had a real haunty look to them that reminded me of something that I couldn't quite put my finger on.

I asked my passenger about the tall poles and streamers and what their purpose was. He explained that the streamers were intended to resemble fire and were supposed to frighten the birds in the hopes of keeping them from completely destroying the year's grape harvest. Outside of that exchange and a few historical facts he offered regarding a couple of the areas we drove through, we didn't have much to say to each other. All and all it was a very quite ride.

Finally, he broke the niggling silence and explained to me that he was especially grateful that I hadn't asked him to ride the filly at the show. "Better you than me" he said then grinned. He started explaining all the reasons he thought it would not ever work with Kitty. She had a bad start and those kinds of horses are never any good. She had been handled far too much and on and on he went. I can't really say when I noticed that his voice had begun to fade, all at once the flashing streamers and the shimmering heat mirages had once again caught my eye.

This time they began to move and shift into and out of forms that were barely recognizable, then just as suddenly I could see war lances being shaken and held high aloft in the hands of painted warriors riding all out on colorful Appaloosa war horses. They raced along the vineyards, just yards off the side of the highway and I swear, I could hear their war hoops as they urged us on. The vision shook me to the core; I had to fight back the tears at this ethereal vision. All at once I felt empowered by a massive dose of courage and inspiration. I felt powerfully fired up for the day that lie ahead for Kitty and me. I was absolutely overwhelmed by the certainty that great things were about to happen. I finished the rest of the trip in total silence and never breathed a word about what I had just seen.

Chapter Nine

The show grounds were located down an access road of the main highway. We twisted and turned our way through a narrow country roads that eventually led deep into a bowl of a small valley nestled in the crook of several high mountain mesas. The view was magnificent. In every direction you looked your eyes would be drawn skyward to take in the lofty mountain landscapes. As if this by itself were not enough, the sky was an incredible shade of blue that held a few puffy white clouds, a master's rendition of the perfect summer sky.

As I pulled onto the show grounds, even before my truck had rolled to a complete stop, my friend was out the door and trotting off towards his caravanning clients to help arrange parking and make sure that they grabbed the all important shady spots, it was promising to be a scorcher of a day.

I found a somewhat shady spot under a scraggily old pine tree that looked like it hadn't seen more than a few inches of rain in its lifetime. Luckily, having a small rig the filtered shade would work out just fine. I climbed down out of the truck and walked back to the trailer and opened all the doors to get a little extra air flowing through for Kitty. I noticed that a soft breeze had started to blow, a sure saving grace. Kitty poked her head out of the now open feed door, looked around and cut loose with a loud whinny, a check to see if any of her herd mates might be within calling distance. A few moments later she tried the call once more, listened intently for a few more seconds, and then quietly went back to browsing the hay in her manger.

Once I found the show office and looked over the class schedule, I made the decision that two classes would probably be all that Kitty could handle. It had been a big trip for her and she'd covered the days and miles away from home like a seasoned old show horse.

Both of Kitty's classes were Country Pleasure venues which meant that all she would need to do is make it around the show arena at two separate gaits in each direction. The tough decision was deciding which gaits to ask Kitty for. She had worked at and achieved a beautiful flat footed walk and a perfectly cadenced trot, something that probably could turn the judges' head. She had the stamina and was able to do these two gaits much more readily and for a greater distance than she could with her loping gait. I also considered that she truly thrived on the challenge and loved the attention she garnered for her efforts. I was torn.

Returning to the trailer I backed Kitty down the ramp and walked her around to the tack room side where I tied her lead rope to the nearest ring. She splashed around in the bucket of water I had secured to the side of the trailer.

While I waited for her to get her fill, I pulled my grooming tools carrier from the tack room compartment of my trailer and began the job of getting her buffed up and ready to show. As I brushed her and banded her mane I reflected on what it had taken to get the pair of us to this point in our lives. How absolutely miraculous to even be standing here with Kitty and actually entering a horse show, the here and now of it seemed impossible even to me, who had lived every second of it and felt every nuance of the pain and pleasure as Kitty had lived it. I said another little prayer of thanks and brushed out the braids of her long wavy tail. I cinched her saddle up and put her bridle on. I mounted up and we walked up the hill headed for the warm up arena that was situated at the highest point of the show grounds. From here, I could see the entire arena and watch as the show progressed.

By horse show standards it was a decent sized show and looked to have between a dozen to twenty five or more entrants in each class. The exhibitors themselves appeared to be very serious about their performances and were working hard to achieve what they hoped would be a good go. Most of the riders were dressed in leather, silk and sequins and mounted on horses tacked up in fine silver show saddles with matching bridles. They gleamed and flashed in the sunlight and each hoped they would catch the judge's eye as they made their way around the show arena.

The time had come, our class was being called to the gate. We headed down the hill and entered the show pen. The arena was huge. It was far bigger down here than it had appeared from atop the hill. Now, here we were entering the ring for our first class and I still hadn't decided what gaits I would be asking Kitty for. I decided we'd just do what we always had done, we'd 'wing it', whatever felt right at the precise moment, we'd just do it.

The Judge asked for the walk to start the class. Kitty was plenty curious about the sights and sounds and conveyed her feelings to me as we made our way around the pen. But she remained quiet and mentally with me, so far she was a champ.

This class was a country pleasure class, which meant that the next gait the judge would be calling would require that each of the riders would have to select the gait they thought would present the best overall performance that they and their horse could achieve. Your two gait choices to achieve that goal would be either the jog or the lope. Without any forethought or hesitation, I asked Kitty to lope. Her lope departure was flawless and she felt strong in the beginning, but by the time we made one full trip around the huge arena she was beginning to weaken just as the judge asked for the walk and then a reverse of direction.

This small respite seemed to give Kitty enough time to regain her second wind. The judge again asked for all exhibitors to take their chosen gait preference. Kitty and I had already committed to the lope so were required to lope off in this new direction or be disqualified. Again, Kitty picked up the lope without hesitation, but going in this direction was her weakest side. She gamely loped the arena again and at about three quarters of the way around I could feel the fatigue seeping through and overwhelming her body. She was putting up a monumental effort, but within the next few strides she began conveying her desperation. She didn't believe that she was going to be able to do it.

I kept 'imagining' to her, "Kitty, I know you can do this, just like you always have." "Come on Kitty, I know you can." She 'heard' my words and I could feel the surge of her renewed strength. She continued on around and never once broke gate and finished the class. She had accomplished this feat with as big an effort as she had ever put forth in her life. I was so very proud her and at the same time overwhelmed by the great spirit and courage that lived within her heart. I just couldn't imagine anyone ever mistreating any horse.

Once the class finished the show announcer called the exhibitors to come to the center of the arena to await the class placings and award presentations. As I headed for the lineup another friend near the rail

patted my leg and whispered that she thought Kitty and I had done a great job. I thanked her and pointed Kitty in the direction of the class lineup. I really didn't care what or how the judge saw this class, Kitty had just accomplished my wildest hopes and dreams. As far as I was concerned, she was the greatest horse to ever set foot on turf, period.

The announcer's mike popped loudly as he switched it on, he made a few announcements regarding sponsors and show hosts then finally, in what seemed to take forever, began to announce the actual class placings beginning with sixth or last place first. It struck me that it was nice that the horse clubs sponsoring this event made congratulatory announcements naming the winners, owners, riders and their horses. All the trainers and exhibitors really do try and put forth their best efforts and the winners being chosen near me were genuinely pleased that they had been acknowledged for their winning efforts.

I sat quietly and petted Kitty's neck and straightened her banded mane while I continued to whisper what a fine filly she was and how proud I was of her. They announced the fifth place winner then moved on to fourth. I had thought that maybe the judge had seen what a great effort Kitty had made and perhaps would see fit to place us; he moved on to third place. I expected at this point that Kitty and I were out of the ribbons, but again I never really thought that we would, just being here was the greatest of challenges and a dream come true.

As I continued to stroke Kitty's neck, her eyes began to flutter to half mast and I expected she'd decided that this now quiet, warm place had turned into a great spot for a little nap.

The mike clicked back on and the reserve champion was announced. It seemed like they were never going to finish with their list of winners. More announcements were made prior to the Championship award. We waited and Kitty started to doze. Before I had actually realized what was happening, another miracle was upon us; the mike had clicked back on and I heard, "And our first place award and congratulations goes to Kitty Silverwings and ......" I didn't hear another thing from the booth, I looked around to see if this was real, maybe I was just dreaming, never really had left home at all. I looked straight up at the bright blue sky as it met the edge of the crystal clear mesa and there they were, quietly standing the length of the mesas edge, there were Chiefs in war bonnets and warriors sitting astride their painted Appaloosa war horses. They all held their feathered lances high above their heads in silence as if in salute to the great Appaloosa War horse 'I' rode. I offered a prayer to honor them and Kitty. This time, I thanked the grandfathers for all that had passed. The next thing I remember noticing was that grounds speakers were broadcasting a long forgotten song, 'Fairy Tales can come true.'

I climbed off of Kitty while we were still in the lineup and led her toward the open arena gate. I needed to get someplace as private as possible, I didn't want anyone to see that my face was awash with tears, no one could possibly know or understand why. As I came through the gate, the few people who knew something of Kitty's story reverently hugged me and stroked Kitty's neck all the while congratulating us as we passed by. My friend the trainer, had witnessed our class and was grasping for words as I neared him. He found himself at a total loss for words, it was amusing and amazing all at once. I put my hand up

119

to stop his effort and asked him if he wouldn't please mind canceling Kitty and my second class, he nodded his agreement and headed for the show office.

I led Kitty out around the backside of the arena to a quiet corner, put my arms around her and pressed my forehead to her neck; I couldn't have stopped the tears if I'd tried. Kitty reached around and gently touched my arm with her nose as if she were asking me what was wrong. I too had no words, but Kitty acted as if she knew exactly what I meant to say and once again nuzzled me as if I had praised her lavishly for a job well done.

When I was able to compose myself and walk her back to the trailer, a stranger caught up with us and asked if he could inquire regarding an impossible story he had heard about the filly. I agreed and stopped to listen. He went on, "I heard that this horse was born crippled with no hope and here you are, you've just won a tough country pleasure class, how can you explain that?"

I told him what I'd told the vet, as I had lived and witnessed Kitty's fight for survival, "I don't believe in miracles with Kitty, I've come to rely on them." He smiled and explained that he also really liked and was intrigued by her name. He wanted to know if her name had significance as it sure sounded as if it did. I told him the story about the barn cats and Kitty's apparent choice of the name. As to her second name, Silverwings, on the day she was born a guardian angel had tagged along. This was one great guardian angel, a horse specialist in fact. This angel was so full of care and compassion that she lent Kitty her own Silver Wings. If this weren't so, she would never have survived.

No one has ever been able to explain Kitty or how she has done what she has, but I tell you this, as God is my witness, when you believe for all you're worth, never give up as long as there is the slightest hope, miracles can and do happen. As for ever catching sight of Kitty's invisible Silverwings, I would be the last to tell you impossible, for she has always soared on the timeless silver wings that are the legend of spirit and courage and an undying faith that holds the flame that is the light of life.

"For he shall give his angels charge over thee,
to keep thee in all thy ways."
Psalm 91:11

"For he shall give his angels charge over thee,
to keep thee in all thy ways."
Psalm 91:11

Epilogue

After reading the actual account of Kitty Silverwings' miraculous life, many people may be inclined to believe that dramatic license may have been taken, you'd be wrong in your assumption. This recount is written exactly as the events came to pass. As fate would have it, the story you've just read was only the beginning of what would be over the years to come, a string of miraculous and amazing stories that I've been blessed to have shared with Kitty.

Another real curiosity, all things considered at the time, was that beginning at twelve hours of age and continuing up until her third year, I videotaped Kitty's progress. In retrospect, it has always been amazing to me that I was able to video tape and yet was unable to take still photos of her from the neck down during her first few weeks of life.

In 1996, I undertook the project of editing over three years worth of the taped footage. I managed to condense Kitty's miraculous story into a twenty-eight minute music video and then hired an outside production company who added a few special effects and title screens. Kitty Silverwings, the movie, was then shipped to all thirty-nine veterinary colleges in the U. S. and Canada. It was our most fervent wish that our experience would give foal owners and breeders hope and in the process save foals who might otherwise not have ever been given a chance at life. We are very proud to say that Kitty's video and medical history were added to the veterinary libraries at the Universities of Colorado, Florida and Illinois.

Kitty definitely left her mark on the show horse world. From 1996 to 1998, Kitty earned multiple California State championship titles for her performances in both the Western and the English Pleasure Horse divisions of both the Appaloosa breed and the Open show world.

On a national level Kitty went on to earn year end high point titles along with multiple Registers of Merit (ROM's) for her outstanding record of wins in both the Western and English Pleasure division. By the end of 1998 Kitty and I had earned a California State title that would have been unimaginable only a few short years before.

In the fall of '97 I decided it might be a real challenge to show Kitty in the English performance division during the 1998 show season.

The real challenge lie in the fact that neither Kitty nor I had ever had an English lesson. My first love was training and exhibiting cutting horses. This English idea in horse show terms was the polar opposite to say the least.

While watching a couple of open, A rated English shows in our area, I tried to figure out the 'what and how' I thought the judges in our show world might be looking for in their choice of a winning English horse and rider class.

Once armed with that knowledge, I started working with Kitty by 'imagining' to her, what we were supposed to do and look like. Kitty had always been able to 'see' what I was 'telling' her. Kitty was spectacular just as she'd always been and by the end of the show year we'd earned the coveted California State, All Around English Amateur Horse & Rider title, another miraculous feat for my once doomed war pony.

In October of 1998, Kitty and I made the trek to Fort Worth, Texas and the Appaloosa World Show. Showing in the Non Pro English division, we competed against the best the Appaloosa world had to offer and we came away with a top ten world title.

Owing to Kitty's incredible overall show accomplishments, she had also earned multiple Registers of Merit, (ROM's) from the Appaloosa Horse Club, the International Breed registry, for her outstanding record of wins in the performance divisions of both western and English pleasure.

Upon hearing the Kitty Silverwings saga, the City of Morgan Hill, California, designated a new street being added to the City map as Silverwings Court, in honor of their miraculous equine resident.

Kitty has always truly enjoyed being around groups of people, has always maintained a kind, quiet disposition at all times and can schmooze with the best. Always charming, Kitty has appeared as an official Appaloosa ambassador, along with local dignitaries during official ground blessing ceremonies within the city.

In 2003, Kitty received another highly prestigious honor when she was presented three feathers by the Carrizo-Comecrudo (Kickapoo) Nation of Texas, in honor of her war horse spirit and courage.

Now retired, Kitty spends her leisurely days in a setting that would be the envy of any horse alive. She has her fans and from time to time a visitor or two drops by, something she genuinely relishes, particularly if that visitor happens to have a Coca Cola (her favorite), or carrots in hand. Life is good, just look in those eyes and she'll tell you all about it.

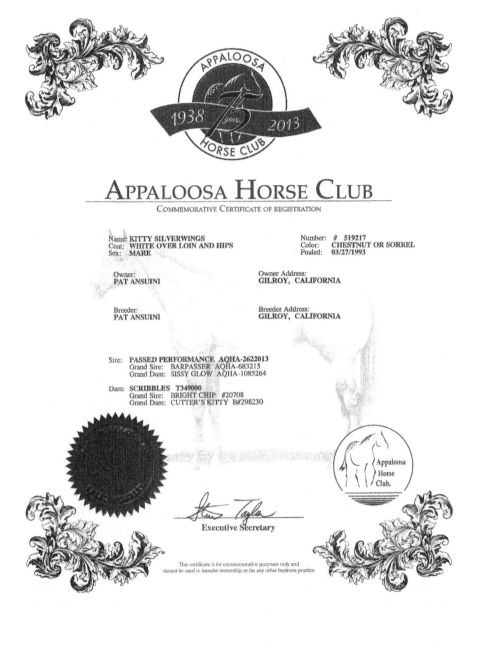

APPALOOSA HORSE CLUB

COMMEMORATIVE CERTIFICATE OF REGISTRATION

Name: KITTY SILVERWINGS
Coat: WHITE OVER LOIN AND HIPS
Sex: MARE

Number: # 519217
Color: CHESTNUT OR SORREL
Foaled: 03/27/1993

Owner:
PAT ANSUINI

Owner Address:
GILROY, CALIFORNIA

Breeder:
PAT ANSUINI

Breeder Address:
GILROY, CALIFORNIA

Sire: PASSED PERFORMANCE AQHA-2622013
Grand Sire: BARPASSER AQHA-683215
Grand Dam: SISSY GLOW AQHA-1085264

Dam: SCRIBBLES T349000
Grand Sire: BRIGHT CHIP #20708
Grand Dam: CUTTER'S KITTY B#298230

Executive Secretary

This certificate is for commemorative purposes only and
cannot be used to transfer ownership or for any other business practice.

128

Doubts? www.KittySilverwings.com

But wait, there's more . . .

Kitty Silverwings & Me,

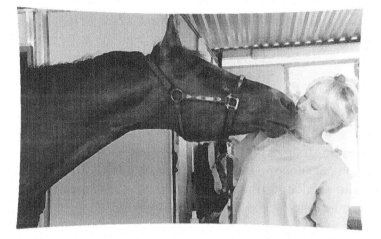

Warriors by Heart

Kitty Silverwings and I are warriors who share one heart. To tell one story, you must tell both. Now that you know Kitty's miraculous tale, I'll tell you how Kitty and I became Warriors by Heart.

In July of 2006, I was diagnosed with stage four throat cancer that had metastasized throughout my lymph system. It came out of the blue; an utter shock to both me and my family. Outside of being a little tired I would never have guessed I was days away from being told I had little to no hope of survival.

I spent three straight months in the hospital, endured radical throat surgery, gut wrenching chemo and seven weeks of intensive radiation.

131

I was struck with a life threatening case of peritonitis, raging fevers and blood clots. The news for my family was always grim.

My husband Pat was convinced that I was slipping away. During the worst part of my ordeal he had strategically taped a photo of Kitty and me to the panel at the foot of my hospital bed so that every time I opened my eyes I would see Kitty and me hamming it up at home in the barn. Every nurse, doctor and health tech that came into the room would ask about the beautiful horse and I would tell and re-tell Kitty's miraculous tale of survival, how she had never given up.

When I was finally able to leave the hospital behind me, it was understood by all those who had heard our miraculous story that wherever you found Kitty so too you would most surely find me.

On the day I was finally discharged and able to return home from the hospital, I was surprised as we drove past the house and straight on out to the barn. My son Marc deftly maneuvered the truck down the barn isle and stopped in front of Kitty's stall. I was helped out of the truck and then supported as we made our way to Kitty's stall door. We slowly slid the door open and then waited for her to realize who it was that had made the special delivery.

With keen interest Kitty had watched as the truck pulled up to the barn from her outside paddock. She stepped into her stall and waited a moment as she made eye contact with me. She looked as if she couldn't believe her own eyes and seemed surprised that I had materialized out of nowhere. Once she realized it was really me, she slowly started toward me and voiced the softest, sweet momma mare nicker in greeting. As she reached me, she gently nuzzled my cheek and neck with her nose, Kitty's version of a warm welcome home and where have you been, I've really missed you. I wrapped my arms around her neck and cried like I was never going to stop. Nothing had changed, just like it always had been, Kitty knew that I would never leave her, that I still loved her and that I too had missed her very much.

In that instant I came to understand that Kitty had been with me every moment of my three month ordeal as I had fought my way back home.

She had returned the priceless love of the three months I had spent with her. I realized that without a shadow of a doubt Kitty and I have always shared a warrior's heart.

So to, I have always known that Kitty is God's horse. I believe that I have been greatly blessed to have been entrusted by God to have had such a treasure in my life. Life just doesn't get any better than that. AMEN!

**The featured photo in this story is the exact photo that I saw every time I opened my eyes during my three month hospital ordeal.*

Extra Special Acknowledgements

My husband Pat, who brought home the greatest of dreams. Who always believed in me and stood beside me during the good times and bad. Who has never waivered in his care or support during my 'close calls'. I shall be forever humbled and grateful to have been blessed by God, who in his infinite wisdom brought us together.

Loretta Goglio, my favorite BFF, for her formidable talents in editing by not letting my 'style' step all over the 'rules'.

Mike Craig, for his outstanding perceptive talents at being able to 'See' the dream. The ability to make his artistic endeavors take on life that lives and breathes upon the pages.

Sandy Cochran Graphic Design, Rocky Mountain Quarter Horse Association Magazine, Production Manager, vNacelle Graphic Designer. (970) 217-5815. Thank you Sandy, for your expert advice and amazing talent in the graphic arts development of this book.

To Ruthie, for insisting I keep the promise of telling our stories.

Artist, Mike Craig Biography:

After graduating from Colorado State University and spending several years as an artist with Hallmark Cards, Mike realized that he missed the ranching life on which he was raised. Returning to Colorado, he became a professional horse trainer and has been highly successful riding, training, and showing for the past forty years.

Mike's interest in art continued to grow with a special interest in sterling silver and sculpture. He has done humorous illustrations for Western Horseman magazine and other groups as well as individuals. His custom sterling buckles and headstalls are nationally sought after and treasured. If he's not playing "elf" in the basement, then he can be found at "recess-time" managing a horse show somewhere.

Suggested Reading

To learn more about the Appaloosa horse and his ancient, legendary lineage or the Nez Perce people and their proud history and culture, the following publications are highly recommended.

The Last Indian War, The Nez Perce Story by Elliott West, published by Oxford University Press, 2009. ISBN 978-0-19-513675-3; 978-0-19-976919-6 (paperback)

Spotted Pride, by Frank Holmes, The Appaloosa Heritage Series, Published by LOFT Enterprises, LLC, 2003. ISBN 0-9714998-2-9

Fifty Years Of Appaloosa History, by Edith M. Stanger, Published by Publishers Press, 1997.

The Legacy of the Nez Perce Spotted Horse, by Charles & Laurelle Cole, Published by Cole Dynamics and Company, 1995.

Appaloosa The Spotted Horse In Art And History, by Francis Haines, Published by Caballus Publishers with the cooperation of the Amon Carter Museum of Western Art, Fort Worth, Texas and The Appaloosa Horse Club, of Moscow, Idaho.

The Nez Perce Indians and the Opening of the Northwest, Complete and Unabridged, by Alvin M. Josephy, Jr., "A Mariner Book, originally Published by New Haven: Yale University Press, 1965. ISBN 0-395-85011-8

CPSIA information can be obtained at www.ICGtesting.com
Printed in the USA
LVOW03s0223260315

432083LV00014B/228/P